GRETEL BEER discovers a diplomacy in an Austrian

DUMPLINGS FIT TO SET BEFORE AN EMPEROR

—OR TO HONOUR A PASSING PRINCE

ONCE upon a time, when kings and princes went visiting, chefs would excel themselves not only in creating new dishes, but also in decorating them strictly according to protocol.

Thus an 18th-century cookery book by the chef to the Archbishop of Salzburg gives beautifully detailed drawings — all in their proper order, starting with a Pâté embellished with the Imperial Coat of Arms right down to one "für einen unverhofften Fürsten" (*for a prince passing by, unexpectedly*). Presumably his Coat of Arms was added at the last minute!

One of my favourite recipes, created for just such an occasion is of more recent vintage—it dates back to just before the First World War when the head of the house of Palffy visited a neighbouring prince and this occasion was marked with—a dumpling. Not dumplings. Just one.

You may consider this a fairly heavy-handed compliment, but not when you've tasted this particular one. It's the lightest, fluffiest dish of a dumpling ever to be set before a prince.

Serve whole on a warmed platter and sliced. It is so delicate that real enthusiasts insist on dispensing with a knife for cutting and use fine wire —in extreme cases a violin string.

PALFFY DUMPLING

INGREDIENTS:

11oz white bread; 4½oz butter; 5 eggs; salt; a little melted butter.

METHOD: Wring out a large tea towel in cold water and brush one side of it with melted butter. Put a large saucepan of salted water on the stove and let it come to the boil while preparing the dumpling.

Cut the bread into ½in cubes. Some cooks neatly trim the bread and cut off the crust. I don't bother with this, but if you do, weigh the bread after the crust has been removed. If the bread is too fresh (two-day-old bread is best for this recipe) set it on a baking sheet and dry it a little in a warm oven or a warming drawer.

Separate egg yolks and whites. Cream butter with a pinch of salt, beat in the egg yolks one by one. Whisk egg whites until stiff, fold into the butter mixture, alternately with the cubed bread.

Put the mixture into the centre of the teacloth, gently shape it into a dumpling and tie the ends of the teacloth loosely to allow for the dumpling to expand during cooking.

Slot the handle of a wooden cooking spoon through the centre and hang the dumpling into the boiling water, being very careful that it does not touch the bottom of the saucepan, to prevent burning.

Replace saucepan lid—there will be a little gap because of the spoon handle but this is exactly as it should be. Allow the dumpling to cook gently for 45 to 50 minutes. Put on a hot platter, remove tea towel and serve cut into slices. Failing a violin string, use your sharpest, lightest knife for cutting.

Cooked in this way, the dumpling is a perfect accompaniment to practically every type of stew.

If you add 4oz finely chopped ham or lightly-fried diced bacon to the mixture after folding in the bread you can serve it with a fresh green salad for luncheon.

SWEET dumplings have of course always been a favourite in Austria— good, cheap and nourishing — particularly when meat was expensive and reserved for high days and holidays.

Thus a meal would often consist of soup, followed by a rather substantial pudding. The Empress Maria Theresa, mother of Marie Antoinette, stipulated that yeast dumplings filled with rich dark plum jam had to appear on the Imperial menu no less than four times a month, because she had 13 children. She bought her plum jam, in large tubs, in Bohemia.

My own preference is for apricot dumplings and when apricots are plentiful in the shops, this is the recipe I use:

APRICOT DUMPLINGS

INGREDIENTS:

¾ pint water; pinch salt; 1 tablespoon butter (heaped); 2 eggs; ½lb flour; about 1lb ripe apricots; lump sugar; 3 tablespoons butter; 4oz fine breadcrumbs; vanilla sugar.

METHOD: Stone the apricots and replace the stone with a lump of sugar. This is best done by easing the stone out with the handle of a wooden cooking spoon—without having to cut open the apricot.

Sometimes, for very special occasions, a few drops of apricot brandy are put on each lump of sugar before inserting it in the apricot.

Heat the water with a pinch of salt and the butter. Make sure that the butter has melted, then turn up heat and bring water to boil. Tip in the sifted flour and stir over low flame until the dough leaves the sides of the saucepan clean. Remove pan from stove, beat in the eggs one by one.

Scrape dough on to a wooden board, leave to cool a little, then knead briefly until smooth. Roll out into one or two sausage-shaped lengths— about 2in in diameter. Cut into equal parts. Flatten each piece of pastry between your hands and wrap each apricot in a piece of dough, taking great care that there are not any gaps.

Bring a large pan of water to the boil, add the smallest pinch of salt and drop the dumplings into the water, one by one. They will sink to the bottom at once—lift them very gently so that they do not stick.

Cover with a lid and bring water to boil again, then reduce heat to simmering. Tilt the saucepan lid so that there is a small gap. Leave to cook very gently for another 8 to 10 minutes—the dumplings will rise to the top when done.

Meanwhile, melt more butter in a large pan. Fry the breadcrumbs in butter until just turning colour. When the dumplings are ready, lift them out carefully and set them to drain. Add dumplings to breadcrumbs and toss gently, at the same time crisping the breadcrumbs. Serve on a hot platter dusted with vanilla sugar.

Cautionary notes: when handling the dough, it is easier to work with unfloured hands. Also, as with most small dumpling recipes, it is always best to make a test by cooking one dumpling first—before covering the rest of the apricots with the dough. Sizes of eggs and humidity of flour vary and it may be necessary to add a little more flour.

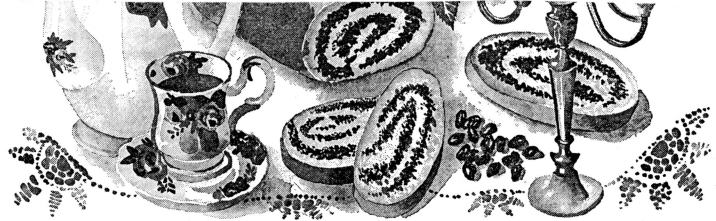

In a Viennese whirl

Frances Bissell goes window-shopping for some vital components of Austrian fare — such as the ubiquitous poppy seed

I spend as long in foreign markets and supermarkets as others do in art galleries. A recent visit to Vienna took us not only to the opera and the Vienna woods, but to the Konsum and the Naschmarkt: strings of smoky, dark red paprika, freshly fermented sauerkraut labelled "heuriges" like the cloudy new wine, bright red pickled cabbage, stubby cucumbers in brine. Butchers' window displays showed every imaginable cut of pork and veal, including all the tasty bits, the offal, brains, sweetbreads, kidneys and beuschel, which we know as lights. What sausages, too — blutwurst, bratwurst, extra-wurst, sausages for boiling, for grilling and for spreading. Dense, pale, fresh goose liver from Hungary was widely available, and, of course, Wienerschnitzel, flattened, breaded fillets of veal. Small versions were served at lunchtime on miniature open sandwiches in the snack bar situated in the spotlessly clean butcher's shop.

The supermarket fascinated me, with its shelves well stocked with dumpling mixes, lentils, all manner of bacon and hams, and a marvellous baking section from which I pulled out a large sack of poppy seeds. I could have had them ground there if my Viennese German had been better, and I had understood the lady at the checkout. This surprised me until I remembered that poppy seeds are an important ingredient in Austrian cooking. Another seed curiosity was the pumpkin-seed oil. Thick, dark and treacly-looking, it is delicate in flavour, the seeds being slightly toasted, and an excellent complement to fine vinegar as a salad dressing or dip for artichoke leaves. It was, I discovered, a speciality from Styria (or Steiermark) where, in the autumn, row upon row of smooth golden pumpkins are to be seen ripening in the fields. If you ever come across kurbisöl, do get it.

Like the architecture, the food in Vienna is a disconcerting mixture of traditional, modern and neo-classical. After eating our fill of semmelknödel (bread dumplings) and linsenspeck (ham with lentils), gulaschsupe (goulash soup), sausages and sauerkraut in the Wienerbeisl, or taverns, we tried dishes of baked calves brains and beer soup at Zum Lämmerer, and at La Scala in the brand new Jugendstil Wien Plaza, a series of magnificent dishes prepared by Werner Matt,

Austria's most famous chef. Lightly fried goose liver on a bed of angel-hair pasta is a good example of the new Austrian cooking, and was particularly memorable for its rich velvety texture.

One of the most popular dishes served in the evenings is schinken-fleckerl, a soothing dish of pasta with chopped ham. In Vienna it is made with small squares of pasta, but you could make it with macaroni. In fact, it bears a close resemblance to our macaroni cheese.

Schinkernfleckerl (pasta with ham)
(Serves 4)

1oz/30g butter
½oz/15g flour
½pt/280ml warm milk
3oz/85g grated cheese
¼lb/110g cooked ham
2 tbsp chopped tomatoes
14oz/400g dry weight macaroni

Melt the butter in a saucepan. Sprinkle on the flour and stir, cooking gently for a few minutes. Gradually add the milk, stirring continuously until you have a smooth white sauce. Cook for 10 minutes, stirring in the cheese, cooked ham and tomatoes until the cheese has melted. Meanwhile, cook the macaroni according to the direction on the package. Drain and mix with the sauce, and pour into an oven-proof dish or individual dishes. Bake at the top of a hot oven, or put under the grill until the top is golden brown. Serve very hot.

The next dish is often served as a quick one-dish lunch, sometimes with potatoes, sometimes with sliced fried dumplings. Any left-over lentils will make a good soup.

Linsenspeck (lentils with bacon)
(Serves 4)

¾lb/340g green or brown lentils
1 onion
1 tbsp cooking oil
½lb/230g piece of smoked streaky bacon
1 bay leaf
up to 1½pt/850ml stock or water

Rinse and pick over the lentils and soak them for 30 minutes, pouring boiling water over them to cover. Peel and thinly slice or chop the onion, and in a large casserole fry it in the oil until golden brown. Put in the piece of bacon and fry it all over until nicely browned. Add the lentils and any remaining soaking liquid. Cover with stock or water, and add the bay leaf and bring to the boil. Simmer for about an hour or so, topping up with stock, if necessary, until the lentils are very soft and soupy and the bacon is tender enough to eat with a spoon. Serve very hot.

For those who like black pudding, I highly recommend this unusual salad recipe. I wish I had thought of it myself, but it is, as far as I know, my father's tasty invention.

Warm leek and black pudding salad
(Serves 4)

1½lb/680g thin leeks or ¾lb/340g ready trimmed baby leeks
½lb/230g black pudding
4 tbsp extra virgin olive oil
1 tbsp wine vinegar
1 peeled and crushed clove of garlic
2 crumbled or chopped sage leaves
freshly ground black pepper
sea salt

Wash and trim the leeks, and split them down the middle if necessary. Steam or boil them until just tender and place in a shallow dish. Slice and fry the black pudding, and lay it over the leeks. Put the rest of the ingredients in the frying pan, and heat to sizzling point. Pour over the salad and serve immediately. A warm leek salad with a nut oil dressing is also very good with chunks or slices of salami or ham instead of black pudding.

Poppy-seed filling
(Enough for 24 small tarts or 1 poppy-seed roll)

6oz/170g poppy seeds
¼pt/140ml milk
2oz/60g sugar
3oz/85g raisins
1oz/30g softened butter
ground cinnamon *or* freshly grated nutmeg
tsp rum (optional)

Grind the poppy seeds in a clean coffee grinder or with a pestle and mortar. Heat the milk and sugar in a small saucepan, and stir in the poppy seeds and raisins. Cook for a minute or two until thickened and then remove from the heat. When cool, beat in the softened butter, the spice and the rum. The filling can be refrigerated until required. You can then use it to fill small pastry cases, with or without pastry lids, which you bake for about 12 minutes and serve dusted with icing sugar. Or make filo pastry bundles or neat triangular parcels with the poppy-seed filling. A poppy-seed roll made with a yeast dough is a marvellous treat for a special breakfast, for teatime, or even for elevenses with a cup of Viennese coffee. The roll is best kept for a couple of days to let the flavours really blend and develop.

Poppyseed roll

¼pt/140ml warm milk or water
2 heaped tsp dried yeast
½lb/230g strong plain flour
½ tsp salt
1 portion poppy seed filling

Put the liquid in a bowl, and sprinkle the yeast on top. Let it work for about 10 minutes. Sift the flour and salt together, make a well in the centre, pour in the yeasty liquid and mix the flour into it. Using a little more flour, if necessary, knead the dough until elastic and smooth. Place it in an oiled bowl, cover with a clean damp teatowel, and let the dough rise for 1 to 2 hours, until at least doubled in bulk. Knock the dough back, knead for few minutes, and roll it out on a floured work surface to form a rectangle about ¼in/0.25cm thick. Spread the poppy-seed mixture all over to within 1in/2.5cm of the edge. Roll up from one of the short edges, and arrange on an oiled floured baking tray with the edge underneath. Curve the roll slightly to form a crescent. Cover with the damp cloth again, and allow to rise for 40 to 60 minutes. Bake for 35 to 40 minutes in the top half of a pre-heated oven at 180°C/350°F, gas mark 4.

First published in 1984

By OSSIAN PUBLISHERS LTD
268 Bath Street, Glasgow G2 4JR.

ISBN 0 94762 101 6

Designed & Produced by
ERIC MOORE & CO.
121 Minerva Street,
Glasgow G3 8LE.

KNOW AUSTRIA
BY COOKING

ANNITTA MOESLI

**OSSIAN
PUBLISHERS
LTD**

CONTENTS

AN INTRODUCTION BY
AUSTRIA'S VICE-CHANCELLOR

Dr. Norbert Steger

"Liebe geht durch den Magen" — sagt ein altes österreichisches Sprichwort. Zwiefellos gilt dies nicht nur für die Harmonie menschlichen Zusammenlebens im eigenen Haushalt, auch der urlaubende oder reisende Gast wieß Gutes aus Küche und Keller wohl zu schätzen. Und gerade im kulinarischen Bereich hat das touristische Paradeland Österreich viel zu bieten, wenn es auch nicht immer gerade "Salzburger Nockerln" sein müssen, die der Kenner als "himmlische Speise" rühmt. Die gemütliche Atmosphäre der hauptsächlich von kleinen und tüchtigen Unternehmer-familien geführten Gastgewerbebetriebe ·in Österreich in Verbindung mit der bekannt guten Qualität unserer Speisen und Weine haben schon viele Gäste aus aller Herren Länder zu Stammkunden gemacht. Spezialisten haben auch das besondere Flair des Wiener Kaffeehauses kennengelernt, einer Institution, die auf die Zeit der Türkenbelagerung Wiens im Jahre 1683 zurückgeht und somit eben erst ihr 300-jähriges Jubiläum feiern konnte. Gerade dieses Jubiläum hat zu einer wahren Renaissance dieser besonderen Form Wiener und Österreichischer Gastlichkeit geführt. Ich freue mich daher über die Initiative der Familie Moesli, das Buch "Know Austria By Cooking" in englischer Sprache herauszubringen, das für alle Freunde Österreichs und jene vielen, die es noch werden wollen, einen Leckerbissen spezieller Art darstellen wird.

Dr. Norbert Steger
Vizekanzler und Bundesminister für Handel,
Gewerbe und Industrie

There is an old Austrian proverb which says, *"Liebe geht durch den Magen"*, literally, *love goes through the stomach.*

Such we have long understood to be the basis for a happy family life, but it might also be taken to apply to the traveller seeking culinary delights abroad. In this field Austria, already well known for tourism, has something special to offer. Who has not heard of the *Salzburger Nockerl*, praised as a "heavenly dish" by the connoisseurs?

The cosy atmosphere in Austrian pubs and hotels, — so many of them family run, — this together with the well-renowned quality of our food and wine, — has already turned many visitors from all over the world into regular guests. There is also a charm for the discerning in our typical Viennese *Kaffeehaus*, an institution, which, (as the author relates) dates back to the siege of Vienna by the Turks in 1683. The 300-year anniversary of this event gave a particular stimulation to the *Kaffeehaus* tradition in Austrian hospitality.

Therefore I am delighted by the initiative of the Moeslis, Annitta and her husband, in producing *Know Austria by Cooking*. It must surely become a treasure to our existing friends, as well as to those who have still to learn about our country.

Dr. Norbert Steger
Vice-Chancellor and Minister for Commerce
Trade and Industry

PREFACE

Eating your way through Austria undoubtedly is one method of finding out what the country is like. From Vienna in the east to Bregenz, the capital of the Vorarlberg province in the west, from the Czechoslovakian border in the north right down to the Yugoslavian and Italian borders in the south, there is a great variety of dishes, many of them still belonging to a certain region, sometimes even to a town or village. The pride of people very often is manifested in their preparation of food at its most appetising. In the better type of restaurant the waitresses wear traditional costume, so that you, as a guest, only by dining there, may already know something of the region.

It was in consideration of these facts that this book was conceived, not only for your information, but also for your instruction and entertainment. Hostesses and guests everywhere in the world can appreciate that special occasion through the creation of a certain atmosphere. Short stories on the name cards of your guests, telling where the dish originates, this combined with suitable background music, and even the way a table is laid – can provide talking points to your introduction of the recipes.

So when do we go Austrian? Well, it is up to you when to surprise and delight your guests in an atmosphere from Central Europe. Of course, there are a variety of reasons, such as a celebration, a homecoming or even the urge to be different, and each can have its own particular menu.

For instance, "Royal and Imperial" dishes would go equally well at an intimate dinner for two as on an occasion for special guests. A birthday party would be splendid for introducing a *Heuriger* atmosphere with all its traditional trappings. Then there is the light-heartedness of the Viennese coffee-shop, – unlike any other coffee occasion which you have ever experienced.

Finally we have the historical banquet – when we dine with Richard the Lionheart – feasting and wining fit for a king!

Naturally too, good food deserves good wine, and there is just the right information on what to drink, to delight the palate with the product of the wine masters. So be different, and enjoy your Austrian occasion!

The Author

CHAPTER ONE

THE VIENNESE COFFEE SHOP

If one is only familiar with the atmosphere of the typical pub or club, it may be difficult to describe what a Viennese coffee-shop is like, and why the Viennese evolved the expression: "To stay in a coffee-shop means neither to be at home nor in the fresh air".

To understand the real meaning of this peculiarly Austrian institution one must know its history. In 1683, after the Turks had almost occupied Vienna, being finally driven back, the Viennese Georg Kolschitzky is said to have obtained permission from Emperor Leopold I to open the first coffee-shop in Vienna as a reward for his scout services during the Turkish attacks.

Coffee was then almost unknown in Central Europe, having been brought to Vienna by the Turks themselves. Bags of coffee left behind when the invader retreated were thought at first to be camel food, and nobody except Kolschitzky paid much attention. But soon the new speciality became popular, despite being called "black ink" by the locals, and for Vienna the *Kaffeehaus* developed a special significance as it became the centre for social, political and economic contacts.

Many people even name a coffee-shop as their postal address; where they also write their letters and read the newspapers, of which a variety is always on display. Those fond of company use it as a rendezvous to meet their friends, play cards or billiards or chess, – or perhaps just to relax.

In the coffee-shop there is no specific tea-time. People meet there at all hours, and can expect to have sweets or light meals as preferred. As time went by the establishments became more elegant, centres for prominent politicians and immigrants as well as famous artists and students.

Poets, painters, actors and journalists met there almost every day to work or discuss their problems. Understandably the *Kaffeehaus* became a world renowned institution, and the main objective of every owner was not only to sell sweets and coffee but to be an ideal host stimulating social and cultural life.

Wolfgang Amadeus Mozart had his favourite *Kaffeehaus*, (today named after him), where he played billiards. Franz Schubert and Johann Strauss on the other hand preferred to relax in the *Silver Café*, where cups, glasses and plates were made from pure silver.

Napoleon sat in a Viennese coffee-shop while ordering the shelling of the city. Leo Trotsky played chess in a certain café, from which he also wrote his articles for Russian newspapers, and when the Austrian foreign minister heard about the start of the Russian revolution, he is reported to have said, "But who will lead it? Don't tell me it will be Trotsky from the Café Central!"

Just how much the *Kaffeehaus* is appreciated world-wide can be seen from the guest book of the Café Landtmann in the Ringstrasse, which is more than 100 years old. The Duke of Windsor, Sir Laurence Olivier and Vivien Leigh, J. B. Priestley, Gary Cooper, Pandit Nehru, Romy Schneider – to name but a few, — have visited there. The better known establishments have become centres of social life, as well as being renowned for the variety of differently prepared and served coffees, cakes and biscuits, without which the Viennese coffee-shop would not be considered worthwhile.

With the right recipes you can create your own coffee-shop atmosphere at home, and offer your guests an exotic speciality.

COFFEE

Every Viennese coffee-shop owner knows at least 10 different types of coffee. You can serve coffee with milk, cream, whipped cream, liqueur or brandy, and either hot or cold, as the following recipes show. The traditional way of preparing the coffee itself (except for the *Türkischer*) is to use a filter. But of course you may also have an expresso machine.

Brauner:
Black coffee with little cream, served in cups.

Einspänner:
Black coffee served in a tall glass with lots of whipped cream and topped with sifted sugar.

Kaisermelange:
Black coffee with milk, to which a fresh egg yolk (one per cup) has been added.

Kaffee Brulot:
Heat brandy and sugar, then add the hot black coffee. Serve in tall glasses with whipped cream on top.

Kaffee Kirsch:
A glass of cherry brandy accompanies every cup of coffee, – can be poured into the coffee or drunk separately.

Kaffee Maria Theresia:
(The Austrian Empress Maria Theresa is said to have inspired this method of serving). Pour two teaspoons of orange liqueur into a tall glass, add ⅕ l. (about 7 fl. ozs) filtered coffee, stir well and top with whipped cream.

Kapuziner:
Black coffee to which cream is added until the coffee gets golden brown. Served in cups.

Mazagran:
Cold, sweetened black coffee served with ice cubes and maraschino, or with rum mixed through it. Served in a tall glass.

Melange:
Black coffee served with hot milk.

Viennese Ice-Coffee:
Cold black coffee poured over a ball of vanilla ice-cream and with whipped cream on top. Served in tall glasses.

Türkischer:
Finely ground coffee boiled with sugar, poured into small cups and served black and very hot. Whipped cream with chocolate flakes on top.

CAKES & PASTRIES

Wiener Apfelstrudel

Undoubtedly the Vienna *Apfelstrudel* is one of the most popular of dishes. It can be served warm or cold, the latter with whipped cream on top — or without. The thinner the dough, the better it tastes — and the greater the compliment to the cook.

The paper-thin dough of this Austrian speciality originates from the Orient. After it was brought to Europe by the Arabs and Turks, it developed quite differently in different places.

In Southern Spain, with its long period of Arab occupation, it became the "pastilla" — a thin dough perfumed with rose-water and soaked in syrup.

At the same time the Hungarians were made familiar with the dough by the invading Turks. They soon developed their own variation, which, in the end, made its way from Budapest to Vienna, becoming the typical Vienna *strudel,* mainly filled with apples, curds or cabbage.

Despite the simple ingredients, the preparation of the dough needs some experience. Nevertheless I have the evidence of a local anecdote to show that it is not really so difficult. One wet afternoon a friend's five-year-old son felt very bored because he could not play in his sandpit in the garden. To stop him complaining, his mother gave him a bowl with flour and water and left him in the kitchen. When she came back an hour later, she could hardly believe what she saw. Spread out on the kitchen floor was a perfectly extended example of an *apfelstrudel.*

If housewives are not always so successful, it is because they lack the time and the patience. The boy, whose only concern was to play, absorbed himself in the kneading process, and ended up by stretching the dough to its limit.

Wiener Apfelstrudel *(Vienna applestrudel)*

INGREDIENTS:
200g fine flour
Pinch of salt
1 tablespoon oil
**Lukewarm water as required (approx. ⅛l.
    or 4 fl.ozs)**

INGREDIENTS for the filling:
1kg apples
50g raisins
**100g breadcrumbs fried in 80g butter or soaked in
    white wine, cinnamon and sugar as required**
Softened butter for brushing over the dough

METHOD:
Combine lukewarm water, salt and oil and stir together. Place the flour on a board, make a hole in the centre and place the liquid mixture in the hole. Then gradually draw in flour from the outside until all ingredients are mixed. Knead until the pastry does not stick to the board, cover with a warm bowl and allow to stand for half-an-hour. Roll out the pastry with a rolling pin as much as possible. Put a large floured kitchen cloth on the table and place the dough on it. Press the dough with the floured back of your hand, working from the middle outwards until the dough is almost transparent. Cut off the thick edges and brush over with softened butter. Sprinkle two thirds with breadcrumbs, either fried or soaked in white wine, cover with sliced apples and raisins. Sprinkle generously with sugar and cinnamon. Raise the cloth and roll up the pastry firmly, starting with the apple-covered side. Roll the *strudel* on a well-covered baking tin. Brush again with melted butter and bake in a medium oven for thirty minutes until golden brown. Dust with sugar and serve either hot or cold.

Sacher Torte

The Sacher gateau, one of the best known Austrian pastries, should have been called *Metternichtorte* in honour of Prince Metternich, who played a decisive role in bringing about the victorious alliance against Napoleon. He took part in the Congress of Vienna and brought Austria to the forefront of the European powers. But when Franz Sacher created this gateau in 1832 as a sixteen-year-old kitchen apprentice to Prince Metternich, he probably lacked the courage to seek his master's permission to name the cake in his honour.

In the same way, he obviously never dreamed how important his recipe would be considered more than 100 years later, when a dispute about who was entitled to sell the "genuine" Sacher gateau resulted in a court case between Demel, Vienna's renowned confectionery shop, and the owner of the Hotel Sacher. The latter, who still keeps his predecessor's original recipe as a secret, won the action and is now entitled to sell the "genuine" Sacher Torte all over the world. But of course there are still various domestic recipes available which were copied and written down when the cake was first created.

Hofratstorte

In monarchical times the *Hof*, or court , was the top social and administrative echelon. Its chancellor was the *hofrat*, and it was in honour of this rank that the *Hofratstorte* was created. In the Austrian Republic, of course, there is nowadays no such function, yet the title was retained, and is still one of the highest ranks to which a civil servant can aspire. They say in jest, "What is it, more than anything else, an Austrian would like to be? To belong as a child to the Vienna Boys Choir, to grow up a Lippizaner in the Spanish Riding School, and to retire as a *Hofrat!*"

Curiously enough, there are now two titles in existence, — the *wirklicher Hofrat*, or Real Court Chancellor, and the *unwirklicher Hofrat*, or Unreal Court Chancellor. It took me a long time to find the difference. Apparently there is no distinction in the matter of rank, but the *wirklicher Hofrat* commands a higher salary.

Sacher Torte *(Sacher Gateau)*

INGREDIENTS:
140g butter
140g sugar
140g melted chocolate
120g flour
6 egg yolks
6 egg whites
Apricot jam
Chocolate icing

METHOD:
Cream butter, chocolate and sugar until fluffy, and add egg yolks one at a time. Whisk the egg whites until very stiff, and fold carefully into the mixture, at the same time adding in the flour. Sprinkle a well-buttered round cake tin with flour, place the cake mixture within, and bake in a medium oven for 1½ hours. Remove from oven and invert onto a platter. When cold, brush over with apricot jam, which can be mixed with water when too thick. Cover with chocolate icing and serve with whipped cream.

Hofratstorte *(Court Chancellor's gateau)*

INGREDIENTS:
210g butter
2 eggs
3 egg yolks
210g castor sugar
210g ground unblanched almonds
50g biscuit crumbs
Butter and flour for the cake tin
100g red currant jam
Some warmed red currant jam as an extra

METHOD:
Cream butter and sugar, and stir in eggs and egg yolks gradually. Beat until fluffy. Finally add almonds and biscuit crumbs. Spread half of the mixture into a greased and floured round cake tin. In the original recipe the mixture is then covered with an *Oblate*, a round sugared wafer. If such a wafer is not obtainable, you can use ice cream wafers trimmed to size instead. Spread the wafer with red currant jam, top with another wafer and cover with the remaining cake mixture. Bake in a medium oven for about 45-50 minutes. Leave to cool on a rack, then cover with warmed red currant jam, leave to dry, and cover with lemon icing.

A cake for a defeated Emperor, a victorious Tzar and a modest Prince

After his fall Napoleon left the disposition of his empire to the four powers who had overthrown him, – Austria, Russia, Prussia and Great Britain. But all Europe sent its most important statesmen to Vienna to decide the future of the conquered countries, and a host of courtiers and beautiful ladies joined them to enjoy the magnificent hospitality of the Austrian Court. Thus the social side of the Vienna Congress made a greater impression on the period than the political results. A conference which had been convened merely to ratify the decisions of the four powers lasted almost 6 months, amongst a riot of feasting and dancing. In fact the Dancing Congress became a part of history, and an army of cooks was recruited to charm it with the most delicious food.

The Viennese had a joke which ran, "The Tsar Alexander, he loves for all; Maximilian of Bavaria, he drinks for all; Frederick of Württemberg, he eats for all; and our Emperor Francis, he *pays* for it all!"

There was a long-running dispute as to rank and precedence, to such an extent that an exasperated chronicler was given to remark that there would at least be no problem with the ladies if precedence was given on grounds of age, – since on that basis none would want to take it.

The cooks obviously had similar problems as to whom they should honour with their specialities. The following recipes are named after three prominent participants, – Tsar Alexander as the Adonis of the event, the Austrian Prince Metternich as the host, (his cake is modest, yet delicious), and (defeated but not forgotten), the deposed Emperor Napoleon.

Napoleontorte *(Gateau à la Napoleon)*

INGREDIENTS:
280g butter
280g sugar
6 eggs
280g blanched ground almonds or walnuts
1 tablespoon cinnamon
75g grated chocolate
3 tablespoons breadcrumbs
Jam for filling
Vanilla icing

METHOD:
Cream the butter, then gradually add sugar and egg yolks, and beat until fluffy. Stir in the ground almonds, cinnamon and grated chocolate. Then carefully add alternately the stiffly whisked egg whites and the breadcrumbs. Place the mixture in a greased and floured round cake mould, and bake in a medium oven for 65-75 minutes.

Leave to get cold, then cut the gateau horizontally into two halves, spread the lower half with jam to taste, and put the two halves together again. Cover with vanilla icing.

Tsar Alexander Torte *(Russian gateau)*

INGREDIENTS:
14 egg yolks
7 egg whites
320g chocolate
500g butter
2½ cups castor sugar
6 level teaspoons breadcrumbs
5–6 tablespoons rum

METHOD:
Cream butter and sugar for at least 10 minutes until very fluffy. Add egg yolks one at a time, beating constantly. Soften the chocolate, add the rum and allow to cool. Add the chocolate to the cake mixture. Beat again, then divide into two equal parts.

Refrigerate one part. To the other part add the breadcrumbs, and carefully stir in the stiffly whisked egg whites with a kitchen spoon. Bake in a well-greased and floured round cake mould in a cool/medium oven for about 40 minutes. Remove from oven and leave to get cold. Then top with the other part and store in refrigerator. The longer the gateau is kept, the better it gets.

Metternichschnitten *(Cake à la Metternich)*

INGREDIENTS:
3 eggs
Butter, flour and sugar each equal
    to the weight of 3 eggs
Chopped unblanched almonds
Granulated sugar for sprinkling

METHOD:
Cream butter, then gradually add sugar and egg yolks and stir until fluffy. With a kitchen spoon carefully stir in alternately the flour and stiffly whisked egg whites. Spread the mixture on a well-greased and floured tin. Sprinkle generously with chopped almonds and granulated sugar so that the surface of the cake mixture is completely covered. Bake in a medium oven for about 30 minutes, leave to cool and cut into rectangles.

Gugelhupf Imperial

The Gugelhupf in all its variations typifies not only the general coffee-shop atmosphere, but also the usual coffee break of an average household, which the Austrians call *Jause*. The Gugelhupf will also be found – together with the gateau – on a table laid for a children's birthday party or for a leisurely Sunday breakfast, where it will be served with Melange coffee.

The special pyramid mould for the Gugelhupf, formerly made of copper, hangs on the kitchen wall of every household. Today very pretty moulds made of ovenware pottery are available, and make useful souvenirs. But of course any normal ring mould will do just as well for this recipe.

Gugelhupf Imperial *(Pyramid Cake)*

INGREDIENTS:
120g butter
4 egg yolks
2 egg whites
120g sugar
2 tablespoons rum
1 packet vanilla sugar
250g flour
½ packet baking powder
50g raisins

METHOD:
Beat butter, sugar, vanilla sugar, egg yolks and rum until fluffy. Stir in raisins. Combine flour and baking powder and add alternately with the stiffly whisked whites of the eggs. Place the mixture in a well-greased and floured mould and bake in a medium oven for 45-55 minutes. Invert on a platter and dust with powdered sugar.

Gugelhupf Imperial *(pyramid cake)*,
background.
Ischler Krapferl *(Biscuits Ischl style)*
foreground.

THE GARTENKAFFEE

After the success of the traditional coffee-shop of the last century, the *Gartenkaffee* or garden coffee-shop made its appearance, and became very popular. All Vienna met there. Either a small orchestra or a military band provided the right background and dancing music. Two famous conductors and composers who started their careers playing in the *Gartenkaffee* were Joseph Lanner and Johann Strauss, the father of the waltz king.

In fact it was Joseph Lanner who created the waltz music. Johann Strauss, who was then a member of his orchestra, later made the Viennese waltz renowned when he toured Europe, conducting an orchestra with which he visited Great Britain in 1883.

The following four recipes, the *Mohnstrudel* (poppy seed cake), the *Biskuitroulade* (sponge mixture filled with jam), and 2 fruit cakes are ideal for this type of *Gartenkaffee,* and of course for parties arranged in your own garden. They are not too rich for a warm sunny afternoon, nor will the icing or the cream melt away. *Mazagran* or *Einspänner* will compliment the fruit cakes, *Kapuziner* the sponge mixture and poppy seed cake. Viennese ice-coffee can be served as an extra.

Mohnstrudel (yeast cake with poppy-seed filling), right.
Golatschen (butterleaf pastry with filling), left background.

Mohnstrudel *(Poppy seed cake)*

INGREDIENTS:
500g flour
200g butter
20g yeast
3 egg yolks
3 tablespoons sugar
Pinch of salt
2–3 tablespoons cream
Lukewarm milk as required

METHOD:
Dissolve the yeast in some lukewarm milk and allow to rise. Place the flour on a board, crumble the butter into it, add salt, egg yolks, the risen yeast, cream and milk as required. Knead thoroughly until the dough does not stick to the board. Cover with a warm bowl and allow to stand for a short while. Divide the dough into two equal parts and roll these out until each is a finger in girth. Spread with filling and roll up firmly. Place the two *strudels* on a baking tin, allow to rise once more and bake for 30–40 minutes in a medium oven until golden brown. Dust with powdered sugar.

FILLING:
Boil 250-300g finely ground poppy seed in ¼l. (approx. 9fl.ozs) milk, add 80g sugar, 50g raisins, 1 tablespoon rum and some cinnamon. Allow to cool before using.

Biskuitroulade *(Sponge mixture filled with jam)*

INGREDIENTS:
5 eggs
140g sugar
120g flour
Jam for filling

METHOD:
Beat egg yolks and sugar until fluffy. Whisk the egg whites until stiff. Add the mixture and cautiously stir in the flour with a tablespoon. Place the sponge mixture on a paper-lined baking tin, so that it is about ¼inch thick. Bake in a rather hot oven for 12–15 minutes.

Dust a cloth lightly with powdered sugar, invert the warm sponge mixture on to it and remove the paper (using cold water if necessary). Spread with jam and roll up tightly.

Ribisel-oder Heidelbeerkuchen
(Red currant or bilberry cake)

INGREDIENTS:
80g sugar
120g butter
180g flour
1 egg yolk
500g red or black currants (or bilberries)
150g sifted sugar
4 egg whites
**¹⁄₁₀l. (approx. 3½ fl.ozs) water, mixed with
   2 tablespoons starch-flour**
Some currant or bilberry jam

METHOD:

On a board rub butter and flour together, add the sugar and egg yolk and knead into a dough. Leave to stand in a cool place for half-an-hour. Roll out the dough until it is approximately half-inch thick, and bake on an ungreased tin in a medium oven for about 15 minutes until slightly coloured. Allow to cool. Meanwhile whisk the egg whites until very stiff and either:
(a) mix the egg whites with sugar and the fresh fruit and spread the cake with the mixture,
or,
(b) cook the fruit together with the sugar and starch-flour solution until slightly soft, and allow to cool. Paint the cake with some jam and then add fruit mixture and top with whisked egg white.

Put the cake back into a cool/medium oven and bake until the egg white becomes firm and slightly coloured. Leave to cool. Dip a knife into hot water and cut the cake into rectangles.

Obstkuchen *(Fruit cake)*
(an old secret family recipe passed from mother to daughter)

INGREDIENTS:
4 eggs
Sugar equal to the weight of 3 eggs
Flour equal to the weight of 2 eggs
Butter equal to the weight of 1 egg
Pinch of salt
Fruit according to the season

METHOD:

Cream egg yolks and sugar until fluffy. Stir in alternately flour and the stiffly whisked egg whites very carefully with a kitchen spoon. Finally add the melted butter.

Spread the mixture on a well-greased baking tin to a depth of about ¾inch, then cover with sliced or whole fruit, depending on the season. Bake in a medium oven for about half-an-hour. Remove from the tin, cut into rectangles, sprinkle with sifted sugar and serve.

The garden coffee-shop as it came into being in the last century. The band in the background supplies the music.

Punschkrapferl

For a long time the coffee-shop in Austria was reserved for men only. Women had to stay at home. Later this habit changed, but up to the First World War it was still impossible for women to go into a coffee-shop without male company. During the war, however, when many women had to live alone, and sought company, they met in a separate room called the *Hinterzimmer,* or back room, where they played bridge. Very often it was up to the waiter to put the right parties together.

So arranging an evening with typical coffee-shop atmosphere, you can also invite your friends to play bridge — but as a difference from the usual bridge parties, you may serve *Punschkrapferl* shaped as rectangles and decorated with chocolate dots like bridge cards, whilst the men drink *Café Brulot* and the ladies *Café Maria Theresia.*

Golatschen

As the name indicates, these dainties originally made their way to Austria from Bohemia, where they are called *Kolac,* which means *cake.* In the days before the First World War, Prague, which then belonged to Austria, was also prominent for its coffee-shops. Bohemian cakes and pastries became more and more popular throughout the Austrian Empire, and — as will be shown in the next chapter — soon appeared in Viennese cookery books.

The accompanying recipe is one of the most popular in this context.

Punschkrapferl
(different layers of sponge mixture, dipped in rum and covered with pink icing)

INGREDIENTS:
5 eggs (yolk and white)
140g sugar
120g flour
Jam as required
Some drops raspberry juice

METHOD:
Cream egg yolks, add sugar until fluffy. Beat egg whites until stiff. Add to the mixture and stir into flour. Grease and flour a baking tin and pour in the sponge mixture, so that it is approximately half-an-inch thick. Bake rather quickly for about 15 minutes in a medium/hot oven. When cold, cut out small discs of about 2½inch diameter. Soak the remaining sponge mixture (approximately one third) in rum, and mix with some drops of raspberry juice and 1 or 2 tablespoons breadcrumbs also soaked in rum. Spread the discs with jam and form sandwiches with the rum mixture layered in between. Finally cover with pink icing.

The pink icing can be bought, or made with:
1 teacup icing sugar
1 or 2 egg whites
Some drops of rum and orange juice

Beat the ingredients until stiff, with a few drops of raspberry juice for colouring.

Golatschen
(Butterleaf pastry filled with cottage cheese or plum jam)

INGREDIENTS:
(a)   200g flour
Pinch salt
Water and oil as for Apfelstrudel
(b)   Extra 250g butter
70g fine flour

INGREDIENTS for the filling:
Either plum jam or:
200g curd (cottage cheese passed through a sieve mixed with 2 egg yolks, 1 or 2 tablespoons soft cream and sugar as required).

METHOD:
(a)   Make a dough the same as for the *Apfelstrudel,* but with cold water, and allow to stand in a cool place for at least an hour.

(b) Meanwhile knead 250g butter and 70g fine flour together, shape into a block and store in refrigerator.

Roll the *Strudel* dough (a) into a square, place the pastry cube (b) in the middle, wrap it up in the dough and roll out again. Fold up and roll out again, repeating this several times.

When the dough is about eighth to quarter inch thick, cut into pieces approximately 8 inches square. Put a tablespoon of filling in the middle of each piece, fold up by putting the corners to the centre. Brush over with egg yolk and bake in a medium oven until golden brown.

Pressburger Nussbeugel

It is very difficult to be certain whether this delicious croissant is of Hungarian, Austrian or Slovak origin. In fact it still provides a common bond for these three countries because of the town after which it is named, and where it is said to have originated. Situated on the left bank of the Danube, about 60 kilometres from Vienna, the border town known as Bratislava to the Slovaks and Pozsony to the Hungarians, was inhabited for centuries by a 60 per cent majority of German-speaking Austrians, who called it Pressburg, — this notwithstanding that for more than two hundred years it was the capital of Hungary, and the Hungarian coronation of the Hapsburg rulers took place in its Gothic cathedral.

A special railway connected Vienna to Pressburg, which made it very popular with the Viennese, who would spend their Sunday afternoons in the park lands around Pressburg before refreshing themselves at the coffee shops. With the foundation of the first Czechoslovak Republic after World War I, Pressburg finally became the regional Slovak capital, which it remains to this day.

Pressburger Nussbeugel
(Croissants with nut filling)

INGREDIENTS:
220g flour
120g butter
50g sugar
20g yeast
Pinch of salt
1–2 tablespoons milk
2 egg yolks

INGREDIENTS for the filling:
200g grated nuts
¼l. (approx. 9fl. ozs) milk
60g sugar
Cinnamon
1 tablespoon rum

METHOD:
Work all ingredients for the dough together except one egg yolk, which is needed for brushing over. Knead to a firm, smooth dough and allow to stand for half-an-hour. Roll out to between half and three-quarter inch thickness, and cut into rectangles of about 6 inches by 3. Place a small heap of filling in the middle of each, roll up like a tube, pressing the ends tightly. Form each piece into a horseshoe-shape, with bulging centres and tapered ends. Place them on a greased baking tin, brush over with egg yolk and allow to stand in a warm place to rise. Bake in a medium oven until golden brown.

Method for the filling:
Boil the milk and stir in the other ingredients. Allow the milk to be absorbed, cool and use.

Punschkrapferl *(sponge-mixture with rum),*
left
Pressburger Nussbeugel *(croissants with nut filling),* right foreground.
Biskuitroulade *(sponge-mixture filled with jam or whipped cream),* right background.

Wiener Faschingskrapfen

In Austria doughnut-making is associated mainly with the carnival, a type of entertainment which is still very popular. The story goes that Austria's Empress Maria Theresa, a year after she ascended the throne at 23, had a most memorable carnival. When she was exhorted by her tutor not to forget her Imperial duties, she answered smilingly, "Exhort me again at the beginning of Lent".

The Viennese carnival is mentioned in the city's records as early as 1465. People then – as in Venice – danced through the streets in fancy dress and masks. In the 18th century this changed. Carnival activities tended to leave the streets and frequent the ballrooms and taverns – according to one's social background. The custom still exists, culminating in the Vienna Opera Ball. But through all the changes the Viennese doughnut, – as ancient as the carnival itself, – has alone been resistant to change.

Because doughnuts taste best on the day they are made, they are ideal for carnival parties. Whenever I have served them on such occasions, there were none left over.

Wiener Faschingskrapfen *(Viennese doughnuts)*

INGREDIENTS:

300g flour
6 egg yolks
60g sugar
1 packet vanilla sugar
⅛l. (approx. 4½fl. ozs) half-whipped cream
Pinch of salt
15g yeast
Milk as required
1 tablespoon rum
Apricot jam for the filling
Cooking fat

METHOD:

Crumble yeast into a bowl and mix with 1 tablespoon sugar. Add 1 to 2 tablespoons flour and stir in some lukewarm milk. Allow to stand until the yeast rises.

Combine cream, egg yolks, the remaining sugar and vanilla sugar and beat until light. Sieve the flour (slightly warmed) into a heated bowl, add the risen yeast mixture in a hole in the middle of the flour, and thoroughly stir in the egg-cream-sugar mixture. Knead the dough well, cover and allow to stand in a warm place.

Place the risen dough on a floured board and roll out until it is about ¼ inch thick. Cut out 40 discs with a pastry cutter. Place apricot jam in the middle of every second disc, cover with an empty disc and press lightly together. With a slightly smaller cutter, now cut out the actual doughnuts, put them on a warm floured cloth, cover with a second cloth and allow to stand in a warm place.

Next drop the doughnuts in hot fat, deep enough for them to float. When golden brown, turn and cook the other sides. Allow to drain on a sieve, and sprinkle generously with powdered sugar.

k + k

IMPERIAL AND ROYAL DISHES

The Vienna *Fiaker* in front of the Imperial Palace.

"Like a river, everything flows," said Heraklites two-and-a-half thousand years ago. "Nothing remains the same, – and in the end nothing remains". It must have seemed to him that mankind was like a fisherman, fishing for the beautiful things which the river of time would carry away. Remnants of the past – no matter how small they might be – still create an atmosphere, and we might flutter through a city like butterflies, fascinated by its colours and its scents. New York, London, Rome, Paris, – each is that little bit different.

So what attracts the foreigner to Vienna? Certainly not the modern city with its skyscrapers and heavy traffic! Sunday Times correspondent Richie McEwan found the phrase for it. It was, he said, the unique charm of k + k (kaiserlich + königlich), that magic symbol of a Royal and Imperial past. The cuisine of the Monarchy has become so much a part of the Austrian heritage that a superb dinner can be an adventure through the pages of history.

By marriage, inheritance and diplomacy the House of Hapsburg was able to acquire over the centuries not only the German Imperial throne, but also the kingdoms of Hungaria and Bohemia, as well as parts of present day Yugoslavia, Italy, Poland and Romania. In this huge Austrian Empire, called the Danube Monarchy, with its vibrating frontiers situated in the heart of Europe, Vienna the capital was a point of focus. It had a talent for absorbing what it liked, and rejecting that which it found boring.

The Hotel Sacher opposite the Vienna Opera House.

26

Thus the heritage of various countries with their different languages and cultures became inseparably interwoven in what we know today as being wholly Viennese. Speciality dainties and delicate dishes, some of them recognised throughout the world as emanating from old Vienna, were brought from all over the Danube Monarchy to the capital, and soon appeared in the cook books of Viennese housewives, who then developed numerous variations, often as handwritten recipes passed on by grandmothers, and kept as cherished secrets.

There is a legend about the Bohemian and Hungarian cooking maids, bearing such names as Juliska and Bozena, who came to work in Vienna from remote parts of the Empire, and whose culinary expertise earned them reputations which became as famous as the *Wiener Schnitzel.*

Today only insiders know that the *Wiener Schnitzel* originated in Milan, whilst the genuine *Vienna Apfelstrudel* and the *Gulasch* made their way to Vienna from Budapest. The various delicious sweet dumplings, today a mainstay of every Austrian menu, were typical Bohemian dishes.

Old habits die hard – especially those associated with k + k. Despite the fact that Austria is now a republic, there are still shops where you can buy the orders and the emblems of the "Hapsburg Golden Vlies", – though you must then prove your right to wear them. The Imperial Palace and the Castle Schönbrunn, the Spanish Riding School, the Vienna Boys' Choir, St. Stephen's Cathedral, and the Viennese University (founded in 1365 and therefore the oldest in the German speaking countries), are the highlights of every Viennese sightseeing tour. You meet the imperial emblem, the double eagle, at almost every corner of the Austrian capital. Where but in Vienna would one expect to find a cake named after a title, – *Hofratstorte,* (Court Chancellor's cake), or a dumpling that began with a prince, – *Palffy Knödel?*

It had always been the custom to create dishes in honour of famous personalities, or even important visitors. The decorations were in keeping with that tradition. In 18th century cookery books, for instance, there are marvellous sketches adorning the first pâté with the Austrian coat of arms, whilst the fourth might do honour to the heraldry of "an unexpected prince". A dignitary passing by! Or dropping in casually, unannounced! It was a matter of preparing for every eventuality.

Perhaps for that reason royal guests like H.R.H. Prince Philip enjoy visiting Vienna, and do not leave before having tried at least one of the Imperial dishes. It is said that music unites nations. Maybe food has something of that same quality. The second last of the emperors, the well-loved Francis Joseph I, practically lived on his favourite dish *Tafelspitz mit Dillsauce,* with a modest *Kaiserschmarren* (named after him) to follow. Almost every visitor to Vienna must have tried the same dish at least once.

In the same way, as a journey to present day Eastern bloc countries will show, many people there still consider Vienna as *their* capital, and keep up old traditions, so that we, the Austrians, more than 60 years after the demise of the Danube Monarchy, can find a *Viennese* Christmas dinner in Prague, and immediately feel at home.

Nothing remains the same, and in the end nothing remains? But perhaps in preparing an Imperial menu, and enjoying a glass of excellent wine, we can still create the atmosphere of days gone by.

The Vienna Burgtheater.

CLEAR SOUPS

As every experienced housewife knows, beef broth has to be cooked very gently, more simmering than boiling, to get a clear soup. In former times, when no stock cubes were available, beef broth was one of the most essential things for cooking, and it was used for the various sauces to go with the meat as well as for the soups.

The story goes that the great Ludwig van Beethoven, who spent most of his life in Vienna, once dismissed a cooking maid because of a lie. All excuses and supplications to keep her were rejected by the composer, who stated that "a person who lies has no pure heart, and who has no pure heart cannot cook a clear soup".

The Johann Strauss monument in the city park.

Bouillon mit Ei (*Beef broth with egg*)
METHOD:
Pop one egg per person into a soup plate and pour over with boiling beef-broth.

Fritattensuppe
(*Soup with sliced pancake*)
INGREDIENTS:
70g flour
1 egg
⅛l. (approx. 4fl.ozs) milk
Cooking fat
Beef broth
METHOD:
Beat egg and milk. Gradually stir in flour and beat again. Heat cooking fat in an omelette pan until very hot, and take enough fat to cover the bottom of the pan. Pour in one portion of the mixture, so that it just covers the bottom. Fry on both sides until crispy. Add some cooking fat before you do the next portion. Allow to cool, then roll up each pancake and cut into small strips about ¼ inch broad. Serve in a hot beef broth.

Griessnockerlsuppe
(*Soup with semolina dumplings*)
INGREDIENTS:
40g butter
1 egg
70g semolina
Pinch of salt
Beef broth

METHOD:
Cream butter and egg until light and fluffy. Add semolina and salt. Allow to stand for half-an-hour.
Cut out small dumplings with a tablespoon which has previously been dipped in water. Then gently drop the dumplings one at a time into hot beef broth. Simmer for about 10-15 minutes, depending on the size of the dumplings. The soup is ready to be served when the dumplings rise to the surface.

Kaiserschöberlsuppe
(Soup with Imperial biscuits)

INGREDIENTS:
2 eggs
Pinch of salt
40g flour
1 teaspoon butter
1 teaspoon grated Parmesan cheese
Beef broth

METHOD:
Whisk the egg whites with a pinch of salt until stiff. Stir in egg yolks and flour very carefully. Add melted butter and Parmesan cheese. Spread the paste about ¾ inch thick on a well-greased and floured baking tin, then bake approximately 10 minutes in a hot oven. Invert on a platter, cut into small rectangles and serve in hot beef broth.

Lungenstrudelsuppe *(soup with strudel)*, foreground.
Wiener Schnitzel *(Viennese escalopes)*, left.
Topfenpalatschinken *(pancake with curd filling)*, right background.

Leberknödelsuppe
(Soup with liver dumplings)

INGREDIENTS:
100g minced liver
10g margarine
1 egg
1 small onion
Chopped parsley
Salt
Pepper
Marjoram
1 crushed clove garlic
1 bread roll moistened with milk and squeezed
Beef broth

METHOD:
Fry chopped onion and parsley without browning, remove from heat and add the raw minced liver, egg, spices and squeezed roll. Mix thoroughly and add breadcrumbs as required. Form into small balls, simmer for about 5 to 10 minutes, add beef broth and serve.

Lungenstrudelsuppe *(Soup with strudel)*

INGREDIENTS for the pastry:
200g flour
Pinch of salt
1 tablespoon cooking oil
Tepid water

INGREDIENTS for the filling:
200g minced meat or minced lights
1 small chopped onion
Chopped parsley
Marjoram
1 egg
Salt

Beef Broth

METHOD:
Knead a dough from flour, salt, cooking oil and tepid water. Cover with a warm bowl and allow to stand in a warm place while you prepare the filling.

Fry chopped onion, parsley and minced meat (or previously boiled and minced lights). Remove from heat, stir in egg, and season with salt and marjoram.

Roll the dough out on a floured cloth (See *Apfelstrudel* page 15) until almost transparent. Spread the filling on two-thirds of the dough. By lifting the cloth, roll up the *strudel*. With a floured wooden spoon, divide into equal portions about 2 to 2½ inches long. Simmer in beef broth about 15 minutes.

29

Markknöderlsuppe
(Soup with marrow dumplings)

INGREDIENTS:
1 egg
50g melted beef-marrow with parsley
Breadcrumbs
Chopped parsley
Pinch of salt
Grated nutmeg
Beef broth

METHOD:

Beat egg and cold melted beef-marrow with parsley, salt, grated nutmeg and as much breadcrumbs as needed to form the paste into small balls. Put the dumplings in boiling beef broth and simmer for about 5-8 minutes.

Milzschnittensuppe *(Milt soup)*

INGREDIENTS:
60g milt (spleen of cattle)
120g white bread
30g butter
1 egg
Salt
Pepper
Small onion
Chopped parsley
Cooking fat
Beef broth

METHOD:

Beat butter until light. Add finely minced raw milt, egg and spice, as well as chopped onion previously fried with parsley.

Cut white bread into small slices and spread with the mixture. Fry on each side in plenty of cooking fat, allowing the slices to float. Serve in hot beef broth.

Schinkenschöberlsuppe
(Beef broth with ham biscuits)

INGREDIENTS:
2 eggs
Pinch of salt
40g flour
50g chopped ham
Chopped parsley
Beef broth

METHOD:

Whisk the egg whites with a pinch of salt. Carefully stir in egg yolks and flour. Spread the mixture up to ¾ inch thick on a well-greased and floured baking tin. Sprinkle with chopped ham and chopped parsley. Bake in a hot oven until golden brown. Invert on a platter, cut into small squares and serve in hot beef broth.

THICK SOUPS

Austrians of all social levels have always liked soup. Whether to restore energy after hard physical work, to put a patient back on his feet after illness, or merely to revive flagging spirits in the aftermath of a ball, a rich tasty soup was invariably preferred to any hors d'oeuvre.

In the kitchen of the Imperial palace, beef broth – the basis for all soups and sauces – was cooked in four huge kettles, with the meat stock as opposed to vegetables and spices, prepared in the following proportions:
10 kg. beef; 3 kg. liver; 12 kg. veal; 10 kg. pork; 8 kg. mutton; 10 kg. smoked meat; 8 kg. venison; 5 ducks; 3 geese and 10 chickens.

When you consider that all this required to be boiled in about 120 gallons of water, and that it represented the amounts favoured for a standard brew, the mind boggles at what might be needed to cater for a feast.

Gulaschsuppe *(Goulash soup)*

INGREDIENTS:
200g diced beef
250g onions
60g margarine
1 tablespoon paprika
Salt
Garlic powder
Marjoram
Carraway
300g potatoes
¾l. (26 fl.ozs) stock
1 tablespoon tomato purée

METHOD:
Fry the chopped onion in margarine without browning, add the diced meat and stir in spices. Pour on stock and simmer until the meat is almost tender. Cut raw potatoes into small cubes, add the soup and simmer until soft. Add the tomato purée and serve.

Halàszlé *(Hungarian fish soup)*

INGREDIENTS:
500g fish fillets consisting of pike, perch and carp
200g onions
80g oil
3 tablespoons paprika
2 small green peppers
4 tomatoes
1 clove garlic
10g potato flour
⅛l. (4 fl.ozs) white wine

METHOD:
Rub the fillets with salt, cut them into neat pieces and put in refrigerator. Heat oil in a casserole, add the finely chopped onion and fry until golden brown, add paprika and then the white wine. Add about 2½pints cold water, bring to the boil and simmer for about 10 minutes. Then add the green peppers cut into strips, the peeled and sliced tomatoes and the crushed garlic. (To help peel the tomatoes put them into boiling water for 1 or 2 minutes). Boil gently for about 30 to 40 minutes, then stir in the potato flour mixed with some cold water. Finally add the fish pieces and simmer very gently until the fish is cooked.

Käsesuppe *(Cheese soup)*

INGREDIENTS:
1l. (35 fl.ozs) beef broth
50g grated Parmesan cheese
1 egg yolk
2 tablespoons sour cream
40g butter
80g flour

METHOD:
Heat butter and add flour, stirring until it forms a smooth paste. Gradually stir in beef broth and bring to the boil. Cream egg yolk, Parmesan cheese and sour cream. Remove the soup from heat, stir in the mixture and serve immediately.

Kohlrabisuppe *(Cabbage turnip soup)*

INGREDIENTS:
200-250g cabbage turnip
30g butter
1 onion
Chopped parsley
Salt
Pepper
20g flour
Stock

METHOD:
Heat butter, and fry the chopped onion and parsley without browning. Add the cabbage turnip, cut into very fine strips. Season with salt and pepper. Pour in some stock, and simmer until soft. Pass through a sieve and heat up again, adding the flour and sufficient stock to get medium thick soup. Bring to the boil and serve.

Paradeissuppe *(Tomato soup)*

INGREDIENTS:
300g tomatoes
40g butter
30g flour
Salt
Some sugar
Some vinegar
Chopped parsley
½l. (17½ fl.ozs) stock

METHOD:
Stew the sliced and peeled tomatoes in some stock until soft, and pass through a sieve. Heat butter, then stir in flour until it forms a smooth paste. Gradually stir in tomato soup and fill up with stock. Add chopped parsley, salt, sugar and vinegar and simmer for about 10 minutes.

Paradeissuppe *(tomato soup)*

STARTERS

Gebackene Champignons mit Sauce Tartar
(Fried mushrooms with Tartar sauce)

INGREDIENTS:
Use whole small mushrooms,
   or bigger ones cut into halves
Flour
Egg
Breadcrumbs
Cooking fat

METHOD:
Sprinkle fresh mushrooms with salt, roll them in flour, dip into beaten egg and coat with breadcrumbs. Fry in hot cooking fat, allowing the mushrooms to float. Drain and serve with Tartar sauce.

Tartar Sauce:
Beat two egg yolks and add 100g salted oil drop by drop, while beating constantly until thick. Add salt, pepper, chopped parsley, chopped onion, some mustard and some drops of lemon juice.

Gemüse in Weinteig *(Vegetables in wine batter)*

INGREDIENTS:
Vegetables like cauliflower (broken into pieces)
Celery
Aubergines
Pumpkins (all cucumbers sliced)
   or mushrooms

INGREDIENTS for the batter:
3 fl. ozs white wine
100g flour
Pinch of salt
2 eggs
1 tablespoon oil
20g yeast
Cooking fat

METHOD:
(Soft vegetables like aubergines, cucumbers, pumpkins or mushrooms need not be cooked. Cauliflower, broken into neat pieces, and sliced celery, must be boiled in salted water for about 10 minutes before using.)
Whisk the flour and wine, then add the yeast, previously dissolved in some milk mixed with sugar. Stir in egg yolks and salt. Finally fold in the stiffly whisked egg whites. Dip the vegetables into the batter and fry them in hot cooking fat. Drain and serve.

Überbackener Karfiol *(Baked cauliflower)*

INGREDIENTS:
1 cauliflower
30g butter
20g flour
½ pint milk
Pinch of salt
Nutmeg
2 tablespoons grated Parmesan cheese
1 egg
1 tablespoon vinegar
Some butter flakes

METHOD:
Cook the cauliflower in salted water, to which you add one tablespoon vinegar, until tender. Heat butter, stir in flour until it forms a smooth paste. Gradually stir in hot milk. Stir until smooth, and bring to the boil. Add nutmeg and salt, remove from heat and stir in the beaten egg. Place cauliflower in an ovenware bowl, cover with the mixture, sprinkle with grated Parmesan cheese and butter flakes. Bake in a hot oven until crispy.

Champignonpastete *(Mushroom pie)*

INGREDIENTS:
70g butter
4 eggs
Pinch of salt
1 tablespoon grated Parmesan cheese
1 tablespoon flour
4 tablespoons sour cream

INGREDIENTS for the filling:
150g ham
100g mushrooms
1 small cauliflower
Some green peas
Some butter
Chopped parsley

METHOD:
Cream butter and egg yolks until fluffy, add grated Parmesan cheese, flour, salt, sour cream and the stiffly whisked egg whites. Spread the bottom and sides of an ovenproof bowl with two-thirds of the pastry. Boil the cauliflower and green peas in salted water until cooked. Combine the cauliflower, broken into pieces, with sliced mushrooms, green peas and chopped ham, and place the filling in the bowl.
Cover with the remaining pastry and bake in the oven for half-an-hour.
Recommended Austrian wine: Zweigelt.

FISH STARTERS

From the baroque era up to the 1900's recipes for fish dishes and seafoods were a common feature of Viennese cookery books. In the 20th century this changed rather drastically for two principal reasons. In the first place the demise of the Austrian Empire had deprived the country of its direct access to the sea, as well as isolating it from the countless lakes and rivers, from Bohemia right down to Italy, which had once supplied the capital. Secondly, the erosion of that religious custom whereby no one ate meat during Lent, meant that there was less emphasis upon the special fish dishes so favoured in the Catholic Austria of previous centuries.

In those days there were many so called Lent dishes, mainly consisting of fish and fish soups, – alas! without beef broth, – but incorporating vegetables and sweets; which is why Austria became renowned for its farinaceous food treatments.

Cookery books had dedicated long chapters to Lent specialities and "new creations" proliferated throughout the country. But when habits changed after 1900, there was a spell when fish almost disappeared from Austrian menus. Only the slimming craze of the last few decades tended to bring back some of the traditional fish courses, and the following six recipes are among those which are gaining a new appreciation.

Lachsschnitten auf Wiener Art
(Viennese salmon steaks)

INGREDIENTS:
4 salmon steaks
Salt
60g butter
60g chopped bacon
2 fl.ozs white wine
2 egg yolks
Chopped chive

METHOD:
Fry the salmon steaks on both sides in butter, and pour on the white wine. Place the steaks in a buttered ovenware dish. Cool off the remaining liquid and beat in egg yolks. Pour this over the steaks, sprinkle with chopped bacon and chopped chive. Put into the oven and bake until the sauce is thick.

Serve with garden lettuce and a dressing comprising 6 tablespoons salad oil with 2 tablespoons vinegar (mixed with water if necessary), pinch of sifted sugar and salt. Pour this over one head of garden lettuce.
Recommended Austrian wine: Welschriesling.

Seezunge in Weisswein *(Sole in white wine)*

INGREDIENTS:
1kg sole
⅛l. (4 fl.ozs) white wine
70g butter
Some flour
Some mushrooms
Peppercorns
50g onion
3 to 4 tablespoons sour cream
2 egg yolks
Salt

METHOD:
Cut the sole into fillets. Place chopped onion, sliced fresh mushrooms and some peppercorns in a casserole, add the fillets and pour on the white wine. Stew for about 10 minutes.

Meanwhile heat butter and stir in flour until it forms a smooth paste. Gradually stir in cold fish stock (prepared from the remains of the fish), and bring to the boil. Remove from heat and add sour cream, salt and egg yolks. Pour the sauce over the fillets and serve immediately.

Garnish with boiled potatoes tossed in softened butter and chopped parsley.
Recommended Austrian wine: Neuburger.

Zanderfilet mit Mandeln
(Fried pike perch with almonds)

INGREDIENTS:
Smaller fish or fish fillets of about 150g each
Some margarine
Lemon juice
Salt
Pepper
Flour
Peeled chopped almonds

METHOD:
Drop lemon juice upon the fillets and allow to stand for half-an-hour. Salt and pepper and roll the fillets in flour. Fry in hot margarine on both sides until golden yellow. Roast peeled and chopped almonds until crisp, and sprinkle over the fish before serving.

Serve with garden lettuce, having prepared the following dressing, (enough for two lettuces):

⅛l. (4 fl. ozs) sour cream
Salt
1 teaspoon paprika
Pepper
1 teaspoon mustard
Chopped chive
2 boiled eggs
Juice of 1 lemon

Combine sour cream with salt, paprika, pepper, lemon juice and mustard. Add chopped chive. Slice the eggs and place them together with the garden lettuce in a bowl. Pour over the dressing.
Recommended Austrian wine: Grüner Veltliner.

Gebackener Karpfen *(Fried carp)*

INGREDIENTS:
1kg carp
2 eggs
100g flour
150g breadcrumbs
Cooking fat
Parsley and sliced lemon for garnishing

METHOD:
Gut and clean the carp. Cut into fillets. Make a few cuts in the skin-side of every piece, salt and allow to stand for a while.

Roll the fillets in flour, dip each side into beaten egg and coat with breadcrumbs, shaking off the excess. Fry in hot deep cooking fat. Drain and garnish with parsley and lemon slices.

Serve with *Erdäpfelsalat* (Potato salad). (See side dishes page 54).   *Recommended Austrian wine: Weissburgunder.*

Fisch-Gulasch *(Fish goulash)*

INGREDIENTS:
1kg codfish or sea salmon
200g onions
Tomato purée
Stock
Paprika
Salt
Marjoram
Caraway
Lemon juice
Cooking oil
Flour
2 tablespoons sour cream

METHOD:
Cut the boned fish into cubes, drop lemon juice upon them and allow to stand for a while. Fry the chopped onion in oil without browning, add paprika, salt, pinch of marjoram and caraway. Sprinkle with some flour, add fish cubes and stir in the stock until the cubes are covered. Add some tomato purée and simmer until cooked. Before serving, add 2 tablespoons of sour cream.
Recommended Austrian wine: Muskat Sylvaner.

Karpfen in Bier *(Carp in beer)*

INGREDIENTS:
1kg carp fillets, each about 1 inch thick
1 pint beer
2 onions
2 crushed cloves garlic
Chopped parsley
1 bay leaf
Salt
Nutmeg
Cinnamon
Pepper
3 tablespoons flour
3 tablespoons vinegar
1 tablespoon honey

METHOD:
Boil the carp fillets in the beer, to which you have added the chopped onion, chopped parsley, crushed garlic, the vinegar and the spices. Simmer for about 20 to 30 minutes until the carp is tender.

Remove the fillets from the beer. Brown the flour in a dry pan without fat, then stir it gradually into the liquid, sweeten with honey and cook into a thick sauce. Put the carp fillets into the sauce and bring back to the boil. When boiling, remove and serve immediately.

THE "GABELFRÜHSTÜCK"

Gabelfrühstück
(Second breakfast)

Starters such as brains, kidneys, liver etc., are appreciated in Austria, and have a certain reputation. But in his indulgence the true Viennese differs from gourmets in other countries. His love of soups means that starters rarely feature as a course in Austrian menus, and they are mainly left out. Where they do come into their own is through the *Gabelfrühstück*, consumed between breakfast and lunch. This is the sort of snack that might be served in one's regular pub, and there are also small restaurants specialising in such dishes. The tradition dates back to the 15th century, when it was called the *Voressen*, or meal before lunch.

Wiener Pasteten mit Hirnragout
(Viennese flaky pastry with brain or venison ragout)

PASTRY:

Work 250g butter and 70g flour together, form into a cube and store in the refrigerator.

Meanwhile make a dough of 200 g flour, pinch of salt and as much cold water as needed. Allow to stand in a cold place for at least one hour. Then roll out the dough into a square, place the pastry cube in the middle, wrap it up in the dough and roll out again. Repeat folding up and rolling out several times. Then roll out, and with a pastry cutter cut out discs of about 2½ inch diameter, spread with beaten egg and put half of them aside.

From the remaining half cut out discs of about 1½ inch diameter to serve as lids, and place them on a moistened baking tin. Now put the remaining rims upside down on the larger discs, and also place on baking tin. Bake in a hot oven until golden brown. Use the hot ragout as a filling and place the lids on top.

Hirnragout *(Brain ragout)*

INGREDIENTS:
2 calf's brains
50g butter
2 egg yolks
30g flour
Some mushrooms
Stock
Chopped parsley

METHOD:

Heat butter, stir in flour until it forms a smooth paste, gradually add stock, continuously stirring until smooth and not too thin. Add sliced and previously fried mushrooms, the skinned and diced brains, and the chopped parsley. Simmer until cooked. Remove from heat, stir in the egg yolks and fill the hot ragout into the Viennese flaky pastry.

Rehragout (Venison ragout)

INGREDIENTS:
500g diced venison
40g butter
Some red wine
Salt
Pepper
5 to 6 mushrooms
Some capers
Flour

METHOD:
Fry the diced venison in butter for some minutes, add water and red wine in equal parts so that the liquid approximately covers the meat, and simmer until tender. Add salt, pepper, the sliced and previously fried mushrooms and some capers. Dust with some flour and fill the hot ragout into the Viennese flaky pastry.
Recommended Austrian wine: St. Laurent

Garnierte Gansleber (Fried goose liver)

INGREDIENTS per person:
1 gooseliver
100g mushrooms
Some flour
Butter
1 small onion
Chopped parsley
1 teaspoon grated Parmesan cheese

METHOD:
Cut the goose liver into fillets, dip them in flour and fry quickly in hot butter on both sides. Place the liver in an ovenware dish. Chop onion and parsley and fry with sliced mushrooms together in the same butter, in which you have already fried the liver until the onion is golden brown. Dust with a teaspoon of flour, add a tablespoon of stock and simmer until the mushrooms are tender. Pour the sauce over the liver fillets, top with grated Parmesan cheese and bake in a hot oven for about 10 minutes.
Recommended Austrian wine: Weissburgunder.

Hirnbrötchen (Brain toast)

INGREDIENTS:
Half a calf's brain
2 eggs
30g butter
1 chopped onion
Chopped chive

METHOD:
Fry the finely chopped onion in butter, season with salt and pepper. Add the skinned and chopped brain and fry well. Add the beaten eggs and continue frying until the eggs are cooked. Sprinkle with chopped chive and serve on hot toast.
Recommended Austrian wine: Schilcher or Kremser Rosé.

Nierenschnitten (Kidney toast)

INGREDIENTS:
4 slices white bread or toast bread
2 pig's kidneys
1 stale roll moistened in milk and squeezed
1 egg yolk
Chopped parsley
1 onion
Salt
Pepper
Butter
Breadcrumbs

METHOD:
Fry the chopped parsley and finely chopped onion in butter without browning. Add the finely sliced kidneys, and fry until cooked. Remove from heat.

Mix the squeezed roll with egg yolk, season with salt and pepper and add this to the kidneys. Stir well, then spread the bread slices with the mixture. Film with softened butter and sprinkle with breadcrumbs. Put the bread slices on a well-greased tin and bake in a rather hot oven. Garnish with parsley and serve.

Hühnerkroketten *(Chicken croquettes)*

INGREDIENTS:
**Half a chicken
50g smoked ox tongue
50g mushrooms
30g flour
30g butter
1 egg yolk
Stock
Salt
Pepper
Nutmeg
Flour
1 egg and breadcrumbs for coating
Cooking fat**

METHOD:
Dice the ox tongue and combinc with minced chicken meat. Add stewed and sliced mushrooms. Heat butter, stir in flour until it forms a smooth paste and fill up with some stock. The sauce must be very thick. Remove from heat, add egg yolk and then the meat mixture and season with salt, pepper and nutmeg. Allow to cool. Form croquettes, roll them in flour, dip into beaten egg and coat with breadcrumbs. Fry the croquettes in deep hot cooking fat on both sides until crisp. Serve with green peas tossed in butter, garnish with some parsley.

Recommended Austrian wine: Müller-Thurgau.

MAIN DISHES

Tafelspitz *(beef with vegetables) left*, Spinat Wiener Art *(spinach Viennese style)* right foreground, Dillsauce, right background,
Kastanienreis mit Schlagobers *(chestnut rice with whipped cream)*, left background.

39

B<u>EE</u>F

Emperor Francis Joseph I, whom President Roosevelt once described as "simple and delightful", was known to be a very modest man. He preferred *Tafelspitz* to all other main dishes, and so in fact do the majority of the Viennese. In the country pork is preferred.

It is said that it is typically Austrian to take great pains over simple things. This is true about *Tafelspitz* and boiled beef in general. The more exclusive dishes are made for guests, but it is the boiled beef which the Austrian eats and enjoys himself, together with all kinds of vegetables, spinach, tomato sauce, cabbage, cabbage turnip, French beans and asparagus.

The *Tafelspitz*, as an exception, is traditionally served with apple-horseradish sauce and dill sauce, secret garnishes which make it a really delicious dish, and probably a healthy one too. Emperor Francis Joseph lived to the age of 86. My own grandfather, following the example of having boiled beef with vegetables every day at lunch, died when he was 91, having still a full head of white hair and all his teeth.

Tafelspitz mit Dillsauce und Apfelkren
(Austrian table-beef is beef from a special part of the upper leg. The meat is lean and fine grained).

INGREDIENTS:
500g beef
Some bones
1½l. (about 2½ pints) of water
Salt
50g ox liver to improve taste
½ bunch parsley
¼ head celery

METHOD:
Put the bones into cold salted water and bring to the boil. Add ox liver and meat and simmer for about half-an-hour. Then add the cleaned and sliced vegetables. Continue to simmer until the meat is cooked through. Serve with potatoes, in Austria also called *Schlosskartoffel*, (See side dishes in Chapter 5), and either dill sauce or *Apfelkren* (apple-horseradish).

Dill Sauce Ingredients:
50g butter
30g flour
1 tablespoon chopped parsley
3 tablespoons chopped dill
Salt
Pepper
Sugar
1 tablespoon vinegar
Stock
⅛l. (4 fl. ozs) sour cream

METHOD:
Heat butter and stir in the flour until it forms a smooth paste, add some cold stock and bring to the boil until you get a thick sauce. Add chopped parsley, salt, pepper, sugar, vinegar and chopped dill. Stir in sour cream, heat up, but do not bring to the boil.

Apfelkren:
Grate two peeled and cored apples, and combine with one tablespoon shredded horseradish, 1 tablespoon lemon juice, pinch of salt, pepper and sugar. Also sour cream to taste can be added.
Recommended Austrian wine: Neuburger.

AUSTRIAN STEAKS

When Austrians speak of fried steaks, they mean steaks which are cut rather thin, less than ½ inch thick, beaten flat, always well done, and the edges nicked to keep them from curling up. Of course nowadays steaks prepared in the English style are available in hotels and restaurants. But it is an imported taste, which does not belong to the traditional Viennese cuisine.

Esterhazy Rostbraten

Their loyalty to the House of Hapsburg made the noble Magyar family of Esterhazy very popular in Austria. The most prominent member of the family, which is traced back to 1238, was Prince Miclós Joszef Esterhazy, who, in addition to being a brilliant soldier, became a patron of the arts. He employed the Austrian composer Joseph Haydn for 30 years as conductor of his private orchestra, thus enabling Haydn to pursue a career free from financial troubles.

Prince Miklós Joszef also rebuilt Esterhazy Castle, now in Hungary, in such a splendid Renaissance style that it came to be called the Austro-Hungarian Versailles.

Esterhazy Rostbraten *(Fried beef à la Esterhazy)*

INGREDIENTS:
4 sirloin steaks about 150g each
6 anchovies
Some capers
100g streaky bacon
2 onions
Butter
Stock
4 carrots
4 small pieces celery
2-3 tablespoons sour cream

METHOD:
Finely chop 2 anchovies, capers and streaky bacon, and spread this mixture on the well-beaten steaks. Fry the chopped onion, chopped carrots, celery and the remaining chopped anchovies in butter. Add bay leaf, then the meat, and fry quickly on all sides. Add some stock and stew, keep adding stock as the gravy is absorbed, and continue cooking until the meat is tender.

Remove the steaks and the bay leaf. Mix some flour with the sour cream and add the gravy. Bring to the boil. Put the steaks back into the pan, heat up once more and serve with noodles.
Recommended Austrian wine: Blauburgunder.

Girardi Rostbraten

Alexander Girardi (1850–1918) was one of the most popular actors in Austria. The round flat straw hat which he used to wear was copied by all Vienna and is still known as the *Girardi* hat. Being a member of the Vienna Burgtheater, Girardi was also a favourite of Emperor Francis Joseph I, who once invited him for a *Jause*, or coffee break.

The Emperor is reported to have looked forward to this occasion, because the actor was known to have a fine sense of humour. During the royal coffee break, however, he did not talk at all.

"What's the matter with you, Girardi?" asked Francis Joseph finally, to which the actor answered: "Your Majesty, have you ever tried having coffee with an Emperor?"

Girardi Rostbraten *(Fried beef à la Girardi)*

INGREDIENTS:

4 sirloin steaks about 150-200g each
Salt
Pepper
1 chopped onion
30g butter
⅛l. (about 4 fl. ozs) wine
¼l. (about 8 fl. ozs) stock
50g fat bacon
2 to 3 mushrooms
Some capers
1 onion
Parsley
1 tablespoon flour
⅛l. (4 fl.ozs) sour cream

METHOD:

Beat, salt and pepper the steaks, nick the edges and fry them quickly in hot fat on both sides before setting them aside. In the same fat fry the chopped onion without browning, add the white wine and stock. Put the steaks back, and stew slowly until almost tender.

Meanwhile chop parsley, bacon, mushrooms, onions and capers, fry the mixture in butter and add the sour cream, into which you have already stirred 1 tablespoon flour. Add this to the steaks and continue to stew until tender.

Serve with *Nockerl.* (See side dishes p. 53).
Recommended Austrian wine: St. Laurent.

Lungenbraten gespickt mit Rahmsauce
(Beef fillet with sour cream)

INGREDIENTS:

1kg fillet of beef (undercut of sirloin)
Lard
Root vegetables
⅛l. (about 4 fl. ozs) sour cream
Flour
2 to 3 tablespoons red wine
Lemon juice
Salt
Pepper
Stewed cranberry

Skin the fillet and cut away the sinew. Lard the meat, salt and pepper, seal on all sides in hot butter. Remove the meat, add the cooking fat to the remaining butter and stir in the finely chopped root vegetables. Put the fillet on top and roast in a hot oven, basting frequently with its own gravy, if necessary adding 1 or 2 tablespoons stock until tender. Remove the meat again. Add to the gravy sour cream mixed with about 1 teaspoon of flour. Bring to the boil and pass through a sieve. Add red wine, some drops of lemon juice and 1 teaspoon stewed cranberry. Put the meat back, heat up without boiling. Serve with *Spätzle*. (See side dishes p. 53).
Recommended Austrian wine: Zweigelt.

Husarenschnitzel

In his operetta *The Gipsy Baron* Johann Strauss dedicated an aria to the hussars, who wherever they appeared were always much admired by the ladies. The hussars were originally Hungarian cavalry soldiers who, finding an absence of good light cavalry in the regular army, formed their own hussar regiments. (The term found its way into British military parlance when several regiments of light dragoons were converted into hussars in the 19th century).

The picturesque uniform, derived from the Hungarian national costume, was brilliantly coloured, consisting of a light cylindrical cloth cap, a jacket with heavy braiding and a dolman or pelisse, (a loose coat worn hanging from the left shoulder).

One of Austria's most renowned hussars was Prince Otto, grand-nephew of Emperor Francis Joseph I. His courage and charm made him extremely popular, and such were the stories told by him at family dinners that it was difficult for the servants to contain themselves.

Once, it is said, whilst having dinner with some friends in a private room of the Hotel Sacher in Vienna, – a dinner at which they consumed several bottles of champagne, – he made a bet that he would go through the corridor wearing nothing but his sabre. Carrying out this wager, he met the wife of a British diplomat, who almost fainted at the sight. Her furious husband immediately informed the Emperor of this "incredible incident". As a consequence, Prince Otto was sentenced to stay for two months in a monastery – whose wine cellar would subsequently be depleted of its best bottles.

Husarenschnitzel *(Rolled rumpsteaks)*

INGREDIENTS:
4 rumpsteaks about 180g each
1 tablespoon butter
30g flour
13 fl. ozs stock
100g ham
250g mushrooms
100g onion
4 tablespoons oil
⅛l. (about 4 fl. ozs) sour cream
Juice of half a lemon
Pepper
Salt

METHOD:
Fry chopped onion, finely sliced mushrooms and chopped ham until soft. Beat the steaks until very thin, spread each one with the mixture, roll up firmly and tie with a string. Fry the steaks briefly in hot butter on all sides, remove from heat and put aside. Add flour to the remaining butter in the pan and gradually stir in cold stock. Season with salt and pepper and bring to the boil. Add sour cream and lemon juice. Put the meat back and stew gently until tender. Serve with *Serviettenknödel* (dumplings cooked in napkin).
(See page 52).
Recommended Austrian wine: Blauportugieser.

V<u>EA</u>L

Wiener Schnitzel

As already mentioned in Chapter 2, this most famous Austrian dish made its way to Vienna from Milan, where it was called *costeletta alla milanese* (Milan cutlets).

Austrian Field-Marshal Radetzky (cf. Radetzky rice) is said to have brought the recipe home from Northern Italy, which was then part of the Empire. Its origins reportedly go back to the 15th century, when wealthy Italians started eating meat and sweets covered with leaf gold, because doctors were apparently recommending it as beneficial to the heart. Latterly this extravagant and potentially dangerous custom became so widespread that it was ultimately prohibited by law. Thereafter, as a substitute for the *golden coat*, some clever cook devised a covering of egg and breadcrumbs.

In Vienna, instead of cutlets, fillet of veal was used for the new dish, and for its golden coating it was first dipped into flour. At that moment the *Wiener Schnitzel* was born.

Wiener Schnitzel *(Viennese escalopes)*

INGREDIENTS:
4 veal escalopes of about 150g each
Flour
2 eggs
Breadcrumbs for coating
Cooking fat

METHOD:
Beat and salt the escalopes, nick the edges, dip both sides first into flour, then into beaten eggs and coat with breadcrumbs, shaking off the excess. Cook in deep hot fat (5 to 7 minutes each side) until golden brown.

Serve with lemon slices and boiled potatoes tossed in softened butter and chopped parsley. Separately serve cucumber salad. (See *Gurkensalat* page 56).
Recommended Austrian wine: Müller Thurgau.

IMPERIAL VEAL DISHES

Imperial fillet or imperial steaks, and the imperial waltz, (the Kaiser-Walzer of Johann Strauss) no doubt compliment each other on Austrian occasions. It is no secret that the Austrians have always loved their festivals, – and there can be no festival without banquets and music. In monarchical times, of course, the season started with balls at the Imperial Palace, and the rich food served on such occasions was shared by all Vienna for one simple reason, – that the servants were at liberty to do as they pleased with the sumptuous left-overs. Cold specialities such as Prague ham, fowl, venison, seafood, salads and pies would be laid out on huge tables for the guests at the ball, and because it was too much to expect them to eat all these dainties, the servants generally had a surplus, which they sold to a special shop close by the Imperial Palace, where the general public could buy them cheaply.

During the reign of Francis Joseph I, hot dishes served at balls in the Imperial Palace consisted of five courses, and had to be finished within half-an-hour, – too much of a rush for Austrians, — because for the Emperor, who took his duties very seriously, these occasions were more pain than pleasure. He was used to going to bed at 9 o'clock in the evening, and starting work at 4 o'clock in the morning.

Kalbsteak auf kaiserliche Art
(Imperial veal steaks)

INGREDIENTS:
a) **4 veal steaks of about ¾ inch thick each**
   50g butter
   Salt
b) **1 calf's sweetbread**
   30g butter
   Salt
   100g diced mushrooms
c) **Knob of butter**
   1 tablespoon flour
   ⅛l. (about 4 fl. ozs) stock
   Salt
   Nutmeg
   Some drops lemon juice
   1 to 2 tablespoons cream
   1 egg yolk
d) **40 g butter**
   4 eggs
   Salt

METHOD:
a) Fry the steaks in hot butter on both sides until golden brown.
b) Blanch the sweetbread for 20 minutes in water just below the boil. Remove the pot from the cooker and leave to cool. Then drain, skin and dice the sweetbread. Mix with the diced mushrooms and fry in hot butter. Then blend the sweetbread and mushrooms through the following sauce:
c) Heat butter, add flour and gradually stir in cold stock until it thickens. Season with salt, nutmeg and lemon juice. Stir in cream and egg yolk and remove from heat.
d) Beat the 4 eggs with a pinch of salt. Heat butter and prepare 4 small omelettes.

   Top each steak with sweetbread and cover with an omelette. Serve with boiled rice and vegetables such as green peas, carrots, french beans or asparagus.

Recommended Austrian wine: Weissburgunder.

Kaiserschnitzel *(Imperial fillet of veal)*

INGREDIENTS:
4 escalopes cut from the veal fillet
**   at about 150g each**
Salt
Flour
3 to 4 tablespoons sour cream
Stock
Lemon juice

METHOD:
Beat and salt the escalopes. Nick the edges and dip one side of each escalope into flour.

With the floured side first, fry both sides of the escalopes in hot butter (not more than 2 escalopes at a time) until golden brown.

Put the meat on a platter, stir a tablespoon of stock into the pan and add the gravy to the escalopes. Take fresh butter and prepare the remaining two escalopes the same way.

Then pour all gravy back into the pan, add sour cream and some drops of lemon juice. Place the meat in the sauce and simmer for about 5 minutes.

Serve with potato croquettes (see *Kartoffelkroketten* on page 54).
Recommended Austrian wine: Neuburger.

Kalbsnierenbraten *(Roasted loin of veal)*

INGREDIENTS:
1 loin of veal including the kidneys
Some veal bones
Salt
Pepper
Cooking fat

METHOD:
Place the bones on the bottom of a roasting tin. Salt and pepper the loin and put it on top, so that the meat cannot touch the bottom of the pan. Add some cooking fat and a little stock and roast in a hot oven, basting the meat frequently on all sides until golden brown and cooked. Place the loin on a board, carve the joint across the grain of the meat and cut the kidneys into slices. Arrange on a platter.

Add a teaspoon of butter to the gravy still in the roasting tin, sprinkle with some flour and cook into a thin sauce.

Serve with boiled rice and red-beet salad (See side dishes page 56).
Recommended Austrian wine: Welschriesling.

Kalbsnierenbraten *(roasted loin of veal)* surrounded by Schlosskartoffeln *("castle" potatoes).* Fritattensuppe *(soup with pancake)* left foreground, and Roter Rüben Salat *(red beet salad)* background.

PORK

Pork appeared as a dish in Viennese households around 1800. The recipes were first tried by the middle classes, but in the second half of the 19th century they had become established as staple items of Viennese cookery books. By this time Hungary was delivering huge amounts of pork to the capital, meat of such quality that it merited an honourable mention in Strauss's operetta *The Gipsy Baron*.

Since dumplings and pork compliment each other, the following two recipes, – differing from the pork dishes of the countryside, – are examples of dishes which soon became common throughout Austria.

Gefüllte Schweinsbrust *(stuffed pork)*, left foreground.
Buchteln in Vanillesauce *(yeast buns in vanilla sauce)* left background.

47

Gefüllte Schweinsbrust *(Stuffed pork breast)*

INGREDIENTS:
800g breast of pork
Butter
Stock
2 rolls
2 eggs
50g butter
Some milk
Pepper
Salt
Nutmeg
Chopped parsley
30-40g breadcrumbs

METHOD:

Prepare the breast for stuffing, — or ask the butcher to do it for you. Free the breast from the rib, and separate on the narrow side the upper meaty parts joined with a thin membrane to form a pocket.

Rub the meat with salt, and stuff the "pocket" with the following filling:

Mix 2 rolls moistened in milk and squeezed with the butter, beaten eggs, chopped parsley, salt, grated nutmeg, pepper and breadcrumbs. After having stuffed the breast, stick the edges of the "pocket" together and roast in some butter and 2-3 tablespoons of stock, basting frequently. If the liquid is absorbed, add more stock, but heat up before basting.

Roast until tender, and serve with warm or cold cabbage salad (see *Krautsalat* p. 56).
Recommended Austrian wine: Rotgipfler.

Faschierter Rahmbraten
(Minced pork with sour cream)

INGREDIENTS:
500g minced pork
1 roll moistened in milk and squeezed
2 eggs
Breadcrumbs
Salt
Pepper
Marjoram
2 crushed cloves garlic
1 onion
Stock
Cooking fat
⅛ l. (approx. 4 fl. ozs) sour cream

METHOD:

Mix the minced meat with the minced onion, the moistened roll, the beaten eggs, salt, pepper, marjoram, garlic and sufficient breadcrumbs to get a medium firm meat-dough. (1 to 2 tablespoons breadcrumbs will do.)

Shape the meat into a cylinder, and roll lightly in breadcrumbs. Heat cooking fat in a pan, fry the meat cylinder quickly on all sides, add 2 to 3 tablespoons stock and put the pan into the hot oven. Reduce heat to medium.

Roast for about half-an-hour, basting frequently with its own gravy and adding some stock if necessary. Add sour cream mixed with a teaspoon of flour, bring to the boil and serve with noodles or potato dumplings. (See side dishes p. 54).
Recommended Austrian wine: Weissburgunder.

FOWL

Gefülltes Geflügel
(Stuffed fowl Austrian style)

Roasted chicken, turkey, goose or duck are delicious after having been stuffed with a typical Austrian filling. Here are three different examples:

Liver filling

Mix soft bread moistened with milk and squeezed with 2 eggs, 50g softened butter, salt, rosemary, marjoram, chopped parsley and nutmeg. Add the minced raw liver and the boiled minced heart of the fowl, then stuff. Stick the edges together and roast in the usual way.

Apple filling

Peel and core the apples and cut into quarters. Season with a hint of cinnamon and sugar. Add some lemon juice and some raisins and leave to stand for a short while in a covered bowl before you stuff the fowl.

Sauerkraut filling *(for goose and duck only)*

Rub the fowl inside and out with the juice of the sauerkraut and allow to stand overnight. Then rub with salt, pepper and paprika.

Stew 500g sauerkraut together with 1 to 2 chopped onions, 1 tablespoon tomato purée, 2 to 3 tablespoons sour cream and red wine until half soft, then stuff.

Another traditional dish served with roasted fowl, which is not stuffed, is sprouts with chestnuts. (See Kohlsprossen mit Kastanien p. 55).

Gefüllte Gans *(stuffed goose with chestnuts and sprouts)*.
Paradeissuppe *(tomato soup)* right foreground.
Rotkraut *(red cabbage)* right background.

L~AM~B

Gebackenes Kitz oder Lamm

In this century, (as with fish) kid, lamb and mutton dishes tended to lose favour in Austria, being mainly superseded by pork. The explanation given for this is that the modern farmer finds pig-rearing easier to control. Also the replacement of wool by artificial fibres has lessened the demand for sheep-based products.

However, it may convey some impression of the way in which kid, lamb and mutton dishes were once appreciated, that for a wedding in 1666 a total of 100 goats and 50 lambs were slaughtered. Even in 1830 Vienna was still consuming 100,000 sheep, a figure which had decreased to 68,000 in 1890. Today only 33,000 are needed to supply the wants of Austria's entire population of seven million. But as a reminder of the old days, fried kid and lamb still provide the traditional Easter meal. Also some of the delicious recipes for mutton have survived throughout the country, as shown in other chapters.

Gebackenes Kitz oder Lamm
(Fried kid or lamb)

INGREDIENTS:
150–200g meat per person
Salt
Flour
Breadcrumbs
1 egg per person for coating
Oil or lard

METHOD:
Ask the butcher to cut the meat into neat pieces, small enough to fry in a pan.

Rub each piece with salt, then roll in flour, dip into beaten eggs and coat with breadcrumbs on all sides.

Heat oil or lard in a pan and fry the meat like *Wiener Schnitzel* until golden brown and well done. Reduce heat while frying so that the coating does not get burnt.

When cooked, drain and garnish with lemon slices and parsley. Serve with mayonnaise and potato salad. (See side dishes page 54).

Recommended Austrian wine: Müller Thurgau for the fried kid. Blaufränkisch for the fried lamb.

V~ENISO~N

The Roman emperors appreciated venison, especially in the second half of August, when the meat was supposed to be at its best. That was the season for celebrating the Feast of Diana, the goddess of hunting. Venison might therefore be regarded as an "imperial" delicacy down through the centuries, even though our own recipes are named, like so many others, after Emperor Francis Joseph, for whom the chase was his only passion.

However, compared with some of his contemporaries, Francis Joseph showed a certain modesty in his choice of outfit. Whilst, for instance, the German Kaiser Wilhelm, often a royal hunting companion, liked to dress up in a special Prussian uniform which the Austrians considered somewhat ridiculous, Francis Joseph himself wore a coarse woollen jacket called Lodenjanker (still part of the Austrian national costume) along with leather shorts which had faded and shrunk through long exposure to sun, wind and rain. Thus attired, he had often been mistaken for a common hunter or woodcutter.

Such was his attachment to those leather shorts that when they were finally worn out and required replacement, his servants had to scrub the new pair for hours until they looked old, otherwise the Emperor would not have worn them.

Rehrücken auf kaiserliche Art
(Imperial venison)

INGREDIENTS:
1 whole saddle of venison (roebuck)
100g lard
Salt
Pepper
Oil
Chopped mixed root vegetables
1 onion
100–150g rashers of bacon
Thyme
1 bay leaf
2 tablespoons butter
1 tablespoon flour
Some stock
Tomato purée
1 glass red wine

METHOD:
Lard the saddle of venison, rub with salt and pepper and film with oil.

Cover the bottom of a pan with rashers of bacon and add the chopped root vegetables, the sliced onion, 1 or 2 bay leaves and thyme.

Place the saddle of venison upside down in the pan and pour over it two tablespoons of melted butter. Add some stock and put into a medium oven. Baste frequently and roast until tender.

Place the saddle on a board, remove the meat from the bone and cut into fillets. Arrange on a large platter and keep warm. Dust the gravy with flour, add butter, tomato purée and some stock. Bring to the boil again, then pour over the meat.

Decorate with lemon slices and serve with stewed cranberries and *Palffy-Knödel* (See side dishes p. 53).
Recommended Austrian wine: St. Laurent late harvest.

Hasen-oder Rehrücken nach Wiener Art
(Wild hare or venison)

INGREDIENTS:
The saddle and hindlegs of a wild hare, or
  a saddle of venison
200g lard
Salt
Pepper
1l.(approx. 35 fl. ozs) buttermilk
1 to 2 sliced onions
Bay leaf
Thyme
Juniper berries
Flour
Cooking fat
⅛l. (approx. 4fl. ozs) sour cream

METHOD:
Lard the meat, salt and pepper, and place together with sliced onion, thyme, bay leaf and juniper berries in a bowl. Cover with the sour buttermilk and leave to stand in refrigerator for 1 to 2 days.

Roast the meat in a hot oven, first only in cooking fat for a while, then basting with the sour milk frequently until tender.

Mix the remaining sour buttermilk with some flour and sour cream, add to the meat and bring to the boil. Serve with *Semmelknödel* (See side dishes p. 52).
Recommended Austrian wine: Blauportugieser late harvest.

SIDE DISHES

Dumplings

The dumpling is Austria's common inheritance. As findings from the lake-dwelling era indicate, people even then were covering meat and fruit with a primitive dough, – the forerunner of the filled dumpling.

There are so many kinds of dumpling, – some that can be put into soup, others eaten as a side dish, a main dish or a dessert, – that in certain provinces the tourist is offered special "dumpling weeks", as for instance the *Knödelwochen* in Upper Austria, where every day a different kind of dumpling is on the menu. In the Vienna of the last century, there was even a special dumpling restaurant, which offered nothing else.

Semmelknödel *(Bread dumplings)*

INGREDIENTS:
4 finely diced stale rolls or soft bread
50g margarine
Pinch of salt
⅛l. (approx 4½fl.ozs) milk
2 eggs
Chopped parsley
Flour as required

METHOD:
Fry the parsley in margarine, add the finely diced bread and continue frying until crisp. Remove from heat and allow to cool. Pour in the beaten egg mixed with milk. Add sufficient flour (the less the better) to get a dough from which you form balls of about 3 inches diameter.

Cook gently in boiling salted water for about 10-15 minutes. Before draining, cut one dumpling in half to make sure that they are well done.

Serviettenknödel
(Dumplings cooked in a napkin)

INGREDIENTS:
8 finely diced stale rolls or soft bread
100g butter
4 eggs
³⁄₁₆l. (approx. 6fl.ozs) milk
Pinch of salt
Grated nutmeg

METHOD:
Melt butter and mix with the finely diced rolls. Combine the beaten eggs with salt, nutmeg and milk and pour over. Allow to soak for a while.

Then form a cylinder of about 4 inches diameter. Place the dough cylinder in a greased kitchen cloth or a big napkin, wrap the dumpling in the cloth and tie the ends with string.

Boil gently in salted water for about three quarters of an hour, being careful that the dumpling does not touch the bottom of the pan. (One method of achieving this is to put the handle of a wooden cooking spoon through the ends of the cloth and rest it on the rim of the pan.)

Lift out of the pot, rinse lightly with cold water, remove the cloth or napkin and cut the dumpling into slices.

Palffy Knödel

As with many other aristocratic residences throughout the old Danube Monarchy, the Palais Palffy, home of the noble Hungarian family who gave their name to this particular delicacy, is still in existence, being used nowadays for representative occasions.

Once, when I was invited there for dinner, a Viennese noble told me the story of the initial ball given when the palace was built almost 200 years ago. The Prince Palffy of that day, who liked to play cards for very high stakes, had brought along his gambling companion, Prince Liechtenstein, with whom he had played *Ombre* over the years. When Liechtenstein saw the luxury of the new palace, furnished according to the latest fashion, he was utterly embarrassed. "I never thought," he exclaimed, "that I had lost so much money."

Palffy Knödel *(Dumplings Palffy style)*

INGREDIENTS:
4 finely diced stale rolls
  or soft bread moistened with milk
¼ l. (approx. 9 fl. ozs) milk
80g butter
3 eggs
1 egg yolk
100g diced streaky bacon
Pinch of salt

METHOD:
Cream butter, and gradually stir in eggs and egg yolk. Add the diced rolls duly softened, and a pinch of salt.

Fry the diced bacon, drain and fold into the mixture.

Wring out a large kitchen cloth in cold water and spread it over a basin. Put the mixture onto the cloth, wrap the dough in the cloth and tie the end with a string.

Hang the cloth into a large pan or pot, (see *Serviettenknödel*) and boil gently in salted water for about three quarters of an hour. Then remove the cloth, put the dumpling on a platter and cut into slices.

Serve with roast meat or *Wiener Eierschwammerl*, (See p. 55), lettuce or any green salad.

Nockerl *(Flour dumplings)*

INGREDIENTS:
250g flour
50g butter
2 eggs
¼ l. (approx. 9fl. ozs) milk
Pinch of salt

METHOD:
Melt the butter and work all ingredients into a dough. Leave to stand for 15 minutes. With a tablespoon scoop out portions, and drop each portion – one at a time – gently into plenty of boiling salted water. Simmer for a further 15 minutes.

Drain and toss the *Nockerl* in melted butter.

Preferably served with fried and roast meat with sour-cream sauce or goulash.

Spätzle *(Special kind of noodles)*

INGREDIENTS:
250g flour
50g butter
2 eggs
¼ l. (approx 9 fl. ozs) milk
Pinch of salt

(The same dough as for *Nockerl* but differently shaped)

METHOD:
Melt the butter and work all ingredients into a dough. Allow to stand for a while, then pass the dough through a coarse sieve (held bottom side up) into plenty of salted boiling water. Cook until the *Spätzle* rise to the surface. Drain and quickly drench in cold water, so that the *Spätzle* do not stick together. Serve with roast beef or venison.

SIDE DISHES MADE FROM POTATOES

Dillkartoffel *(Potatoes in dill sauce)*

INGREDIENTS:
750g potatoes
30g flour
40g butter
Pepper
Salt
Sugar
3 teaspoons chopped dill
1 teaspoon chopped parsley
1 teaspoon vinegar
Stock as required
⅛ l. (approx. 4fl. ozs) sour cream

METHOD:
Boil the potatoes in their jackets. Meanwhile heat butter, stir in flour and gradually add stock until you get a thickish sauce. Stir in the spices, a pinch of sugar and vinegar. Bring to the boil and add sour cream. Put aside.

Peel and slice the potatoes and add to the sauce. Heat up again and simmer for 1 to 2 minutes. Remove from the heat and serve.

(Excellent with boiled or roasted meat, fish or hot sausages).

Kartoffelkroketten *(Potato croquettes)*

INGREDIENTS:
500g boiled and peeled potatoes
1 egg
100g flour
1 tablespoon butter
Salt
1 egg and breadcrumbs for coating
Cooking fat

METHOD:
Mash the potatoes while still hot. Leave to cool, then mix with flour, 1 egg, salt and a tablespoon of butter. Work into a dough and scoop out small portions. Form each portion into a small cylinder about 2 inches long, dip into beaten egg and roll in breadcrumbs. Fry in hot deep cooking fat until golden brown.

Every kind of vegetable and fried meat goes with this dish.

Erdäpfelknödel *(Potato dumplings)*

INGREDIENTS:
500g potatoes
1 egg
Salt
50g finely diced white bread
Semolina as required
Some margarine

METHOD:
Peel the potatoes, cut them into halves and boil in salted water. Drain and mash.

Heat margarine and fry the finely diced white bread until golden brown. Remove from heat and mix with the mashed potatoes, salt, egg and sufficient semolina to get a medium firm dough. Form balls of about 2 inches diameter, allow to stand for half-an-hour, then cook for 10 to 15 minutes in salted boiling water.

Serve with roast or fried pork and beef.

Erdäpfelsalat *(Potato salad)*

INGREDIENTS:
500g potatoes
2 tablespoons vinegar
2 tablespoons salad oil
2 to 3 tablespoons cold stock
1 finely chopped onion
Salt
Pepper
Chopped chive

METHOD:
Boil the potatoes in their jackets. Peel and slice thinly. Combine salad oil, vinegar and spices, and pour over the potatoes while still warm. Add chopped onion and chopped chive and stir in 2 to 3 tablespoons cold stock. Mix gently and allow to stand for 1 hour.

Excellent with dishes like Wiener Schnitzel, fried carp or fried kid or lamb.

VEGETABLE SIDE DISHES

Kohlsprossen mit Kastanien
(Sprouts with chestnuts)

INGREDIENTS:
500g sprouts
500g chestnuts
60g butter
Salt
Nutmeg
Some stock

METHOD:
    Nick the skin of the chestnuts and cook for about 10 minutes in water. Peel when still hot, put back into the salted water and cook until soft.
    Meanwhile stew the cleaned sprouts in butter and some stock until soft, with the liquid all absorbed. Add the cooked chestnuts, season with nutmeg and add 1 or 2 teaspoons of butter.
    Excellent with fowl.

Spinat Wiener Art *(Spinach Viennese style)*

INGREDIENTS:
500g spinach
1l. (approx. 35fl.ozs) water
40g butter
30g flour
Salt
Pepper
1 or 2 crushed cloves garlic
Stock or milk

METHOD:
    Clean the spinach and remove large stalks. Put into the boiling water and simmer until soft. Drain and pass through a sieve.
    Heat butter and stir in flour. Gradually add some stock (or cold milk) until you get a smooth and very thick sauce. Season with salt, pepper and crushed garlic. Add the spinach, bring to the boil and serve.
    Excellent with boiled beef, fried and boiled eggs or brain-toast.

Wiener Eierschwammerl
(Viennese Chanterelles)

INGREDIENTS:
500g chanterelles
100g butter
1 onion
Chopped parsley
Salt
Pepper
½ crushed clove of garlic
1 level tablespoon flour
⅛l. (approx. 4fl. ozs) sour cream
1 or 2 egg yolks
Stock as required

METHOD:
    Fry the finely chopped onion and parsley lightly in butter. Add the sliced chanterelles, the crushed garlic and the spices. Cook until the chanterelles are almost tender, stirring continuously.
    Mix the flour with sour cream and some cold stock and pour this over the chanterelles.
    Simmer until the chanterelles are cooked. Finally add the egg yolks and serve.
    Serve with lettuce, bread dumplings or dumplings *Palffy style.*

SALAD SIDE DISHES

Roter Rüben Salat *(Red beet salad)*

METHOD:
Clean and cook the red beets in salted water until soft.
Rinse in cold water, peel and cut into fine slices. Heat vinegar
mixed with water to taste, add salt and caraway and bring to
the boil. Simmer for 1 or 2 minutes. Pour this mixture over the
red beets and allow to cool. Add pepper and 1 or 2 tablespoons
salad oil.
Serve with roast meat.

Krautsalat *(Cabbage salad)*

INGREDIENTS:
500g finely shredded white cabbage
⅛l. (approx. 4fl. ozs) wine vinegar
Salt
Caraway
1 chopped onion
Salad oil or streaky bacon

METHOD:
Boil cabbage and caraway in salted water and cook until
soft but still crisp. (One minute will do). Drain and mix with
the chopped onion, vinegar and oil. Allow to get cold and
serve.
Another method is to mix the drained cabbage with
vinegar, chopped onion and diced bacon, which has been
previously fried until crisp, but is still hot. Pour the hot bacon
fat over the salad, mix and serve warm.

Gurkensalat *(Cucumber salad)*

INGREDIENTS:
2 cucumbers
Salt
Pepper
1 or 2 tablespoons vinegar
3 tablespoons salad oil
⅛l. (approx. 4fl. ozs) sour cream
Chopped dill.

METHOD:
Peel and cut the cucumbers in very thin slices. Salt and
allow to stand for a while. Press out and pour off the juice. Mix
the cucumbers with either salt, pepper, vinegar and oil, or salt,
pepper, sour cream and chopped dill.

DESSERTS & SWEETS

Kaiserschmarren

There are still three factions in Austria contesting the origin of this popular dish. Vienna, as the capital, claims the *Kaiserschmarren* to be typically Viennese, the Kaiser being Francis Joseph, for whom it was a favourite dessert.

On the other hand the township of Bad Ischl in Upper Austria, where the Emperor went every year for his summer holidays, argues that the dish has associations with the surrounding country, and that it was in Bad Ischl that it first graced the royal table.

The third story is the least controversial. According to this version, the word *Kaiserschmarren* is a corruption of *Koaserschmarren*, *Koaser* being an Austrian dialect word for a cheese producer. It is said that they actually created the dish, which was originally prepared in an iron pan on an open fire.

Kaiserschmarren *(Emperor's omelette)*

INGREDIENTS:
⅜ l. (approx. 13 fl. ozs) milk
170 g flour
4 eggs
80 g sugar
60 g butter
Pinch of salt
80 g butter for baking
50 g raisins
Sifted sugar

METHOD:
Melt the butter and mix with egg yolks, sugar, flour and salt. Whisk the egg whites very stiffly and add to the mixture. Heat 40 g butter in an omelette pan and pour in the batter until finger-deep. Sprinkle on the raisins and cook till golden yellow with slightly brown rims.

Add the remaining 40 g butter, turn the omelette over and cook the other side the same way. Then tear the omelette with 2 forks into small pieces and allow to become almost dry.

Sprinkle with sifted sugar and serve with compote.

Kaiserkoch *(Emperor's soufflé)*

INGREDIENTS:
3 eggs
3 tablespoons sugar
3 tablespoons butter
2 diced stale rolls
⅛ l. (approx. 4 fl. ozs) milk
2 tablespoons grated almonds
Some breadcrumbs
150 g cherries without stones

INGREDIENTS for the topping:
2 egg whites
2 tablespoons apricot jelly
2 tablespoons sifted sugar

METHOD:
Cream butter, sugar and egg yolks until fluffy. Mix with the diced rolls moistened in the milk. Add the grated almonds. Beat until the mixture is smooth and carefully add the stiffly whisked egg whites.

Spread a buttered baking mould with some breadcrumbs and half fill with the mixture. Top with the cherries then add the other half. Bake in a medium oven for about half-an-hour.

Meanwhile beat one egg white together with the apricot jelly until smooth. Whisk the second egg white until stiff and add.

Top the *Kaiserkoch* with the mixture, put it back into the oven, reduce the heat a little and bake until the mixture of egg whites and jelly gets firm and slightly coloured (approx. 10 to 15 minutes).

Serve warm with whipped cream.

Radetzky Reis *(Rice à la Radetzky)*

INGREDIENTS:
200g rice
1 l.(35fl. ozs) milk
50g butter
Juice of 2 oranges
2-3 tablespoons rum
Apricot jam
4 egg whites
1 tablespoon sugar mixed with vanilla sugar
30g chopped almonds
Butter for the mould

METHOD:
Boil the rice with a pinch of salt and butter in milk until soft. Leave to cool, and stir in orange juice and rum.

Place half of the mixture in a greased baking mould. Spread with apricot jam and add the second half. Top with the stiffly whisked egg whites combined with sugar and vanilla sugar. Sprinkle with chopped almonds and sifted sugar and bake in a medium oven for 10 to 15 minutes until the top gets golden-yellow. Scoop out portions and sprinkle generously with sifted sugar.

Weinchadeau *(Wine-cream)*

INGREDIENTS:
¼l. (approx.9 fl. ozs) white wine
4 egg yolks
80g sugar
Some vanilla sugar

METHOD:
Combine all ingredients and whisk over a low heat until fluffy.

Radetzky Reis

Field Marshal Graf Joseph Radetzky was one of the most efficient and noteworthy of the galaxy of Central European professional soldiers.

Fighting against Napoleon I and Napoleon III he became a national hero. But as the son of an old noble family of Hungarian extraction he was more than that. He had the attribute, — not very common among Austrian generals, — of being idolised by the rank and file, and was affectionately known as Father Radetzky.

Johann Strauss dedicated to him his most popular piece of martial music, the Radetzky March. And in the monastery of Melk, famous throughout Austria for its library, there is a handwritten cookery book with a recipe entitled "Father Radetzky's favourite rice".

The hero is gone, but the appetite stays. Perhaps this recipe is a better monument to him than anything of marble or stone.

Dining with sorcerers and witches

According to legend, when witches and sorcerers meet in the *Walpurgis-night,* it is said that ordinary people can watch them if they eat special *witch-dishes* before the meeting. The following two recipes are handed down from those superstitious times.

Hexenschaum *(Witch-Foam)*

INGREDIENTS:
650g apples
200g sugar
2 egg whites
Juice of 1 lemon
Whipped cream

METHOD:
Peel, core and cut the apples into quarters. Add sugar and lemon juice and stew in a little water until soft. Drain, pass through a sieve, — or put into the blender, — and leave to cool.

Meanwhile whisk the egg whites until stiff, combine with the cold apple-mixture and beat until thick and creamy. Serve in tall glasses and top with whipped cream.

Scheiterhaufen *("Stake")*

INGREDIENTS:
4-6 rolls or soft bread
⅜l. (approx. 13fl.ozs) milk
100g sugar
4 egg whites
2 egg yolks
50g raisins
50g chopped almonds
250g apples
Some jam
Butter for the mould
Some sugar for the foam

METHOD:
Cut the bread into thin slices and place the first layer in a greased baking mould. Top with a layer of sliced apples mixed with raisins and chopped almonds. Cover with a layer of bread and then alternate bread and apples, but make sure that the last layer consists of bread.

Mix milk with egg yolks and sugar and pour over. Allow to soak for a while, then put into a medium oven. Bake while you whisk the egg whites with a tablespoon of sugar until very stiff. Top the bread cake with the stiffly beaten egg whites and continue baking until golden brown.

Topfenpalatschinken *(Pancakes with curds)*

INGREDIENTS:
150g flour
1 or 2 eggs
Pinch of salt
Milk as required (from 5 to 9 fl. ozs)

INGREDIENTS for the filling:
150g curds (passed through a sieve)
2 egg yolks
40g sugar
50g raisins

METHOD:
Work all ingredients for the pancakes into a thin batter and fry approximately 6 pancakes. Put aside and keep warm.

Mix all ingredients for the filling together and spread the mixture on the pancakes. Roll up each pancake, sprinkle with sifted sugar and top, as a delicious extra, with 1 tablespoon of sour cream.

Wiener Savarin

In accordance with the Austrian custom of naming dishes after renowned people, this Viennese dish was created to honour the French judge and author, Brillat-Savarin. He lived from 1755 to 1826, and was known for his humorous contributions to excellence in eating.

Wiener Savarin *(Viennese Savarin)*

INGREDIENTS:
200g flour
50g butter
3 egg yolks
30g sugar
15g yeast
Pinch of salt
1/16 l. (approx. 2 fl. ozs) milk

INGREDIENTS for the coating:
150g sugar
Juice of 1 orange
3 tablespoons rum or liqueur
Cooking chocolate
Whipped cream

METHOD:
Dissolve the yeast in the lukewarm milk, add some sugar and flour, cover and allow to stand in a warm place to rise. Stir in the remaining ingredients and beat well. Fill the mixture into a buttered mould, allow to rise again and bake until golden brown.

Invert on to a platter. Then boil up 150g sugar with 1/4 l. (approx. 9 fl. ozs) water until slightly thickish. Add rum and orange juice. Pour this with a tablespoon over the hot cake, allow to soak, top with melted chocolate and garnish with whipped cream. Serve hot.

Topfenknödel mit Zwetschkenröster

The legendary homeland of the sweet dumplings is Bohemia, where they are called *knedlks*. They did not appear as an Austrian dish until the middle of the last century, but once they featured in Viennese cook-books, they soon spread throughout the country.

Powidltascherl

This is a typical Bohemian dish, which was ultimately adopted as *genuine* Viennese. In Bohemia the word *tarĉka* signifies the mediaeval form of an escutcheon, and the *Powidltascherl* gets this name because of its characteristic shape.

Topfenknödel mit Zwetschkenröster
(Curds-dumpling with plum compote Austrian style)

INGREDIENTS:
3 eggs
90g butter
Pinch of salt
300g curds
120g semolina
Butter and breadcrumbs for coating

METHOD:

Cream egg yolks and butter until fluffy. Add salt, semolina and the curds (if too coarse, pass through a sieve), and allow to stand for 1 hour.

Whisk the egg whites until stiff, and fold gently into the mixture. Form balls of about 2½inches diameter and simmer in boiling salted water for about 15 minutes. Drain and roll the dumplings in breadcrumbs fried in butter. Sprinkle with sifted sugar and serve hot together with *Zwetschkenröster*.

Zwetschkenröster
(Plum-compote Austrian style)

Stone the plums and cut into halves. Mix with sugar to taste, and stew without water until soft and crumbling into pieces.

Powidltascherl *(Damson pochettes)*

INGREDIENTS:
1kg boiled potatoes
200-250g flour
1 egg
50g butter
Pinch of salt
100g butter and
     100g breadcrumbs for coating
Sifted sugar

METHOD:

Boil and peel the potatoes, press through a sieve, or mash while still hot. Mix the potatoes with flour, butter, egg and salt and work into a dough.

Divide the dough into several pieces, roll out each piece, — one at a time, — until approx. ½ inch thick. Cut into 4 inch squares, and put in the middle of each square 1 teaspoon of damson. Fold the squares to get a triangle, and pinch the edges together.

Simmer in boiling salted water for 8 to 10 minutes.

Drain and toss in breadcrumbs fried in butter. Arrange on a platter, sprinkle generously with sifted sugar and serve hot.

How to prepare **Powidl** (*Damson*)

INGREDIENTS:
6kg plums
1kg sugar
½l. (approx. 18 fl. ozs) wine vinegar.

METHOD:
Mix the stoned plums with sugar and pour over with the wine vinegar.

Allow to stand overnight. Then cook the plums for 6 to 8 hours into a thick pulp, fill into glasses, place in a hot oven, close the door and leave for some minutes, — long enough for the jam to skin over.

Buchteln mit Vanillesauce
(Yeast buns with vanilla sauce)

INGREDIENTS:
500g flour
30g yeast
50g sugar
70g butter
2 egg yolks
1 egg white
Pinch of salt
Lukewarm milk
Butter for spreading
Jam

METHOD:
Place the flour in a warm bowl and make a hole in the centre. Crumble the yeast into it, sprinkle with a tablespoon sugar, add 2 to 3 tablespoons lukewarm milk and cover lightly with flour. Put in a warm place to rise.

Meanwhile melt the butter, lift off and cool a bit, then mix with a pinch of salt, the egg yolks and the egg white. Add this to the flour where the yeast in the middle has risen, and beat by adding as much lukewarm milk as needed to get a medium firm dough. Continue beating until the dough no longer sticks to the bowl. Cover, and allow to rise.

Roll out the dough on a floured board until ¼ to ½ inch thick, cut out squares of about 3 inches side-length, put a teaspoon of jam in the middle, preferably apricot, then fold up and form into an egg shape. Brush over with softened butter on all sides of each piece, and tightly fit one after the other in a well-greased baking tin.

Brush over again with softened butter and allow to rise. Bake first in a medium oven, then raise the temperature and bake until golden brown. When ready, sprinkle with sifted sugar and serve hot with vanilla sauce.

Vanillesauce (*Vanilla sauce*)

INGREDIENTS:
¼l. (approx. 9 fl. ozs) milk
¼l. (approx. 9 fl. ozs) cream
Sugar as required
Vanilla sugar
3 egg yolks
1 teaspoon starch flour

METHOD:
Combine cold milk and cream with the other ingredients, heat up and beat continuously until boiling. When thick, remove from heat and serve.

Kastanienreis mit Schlagobers
(Chestnut rice with whipped cream)

INGREDIENTS:
1kg chestnuts
120g sifted sugar
1 tablespoon rum
¼l. (approx. 9 fl. ozs) cream

METHOD:
Nick the shells of the chestnuts and boil for 10 minutes, then peel and continue cooking in salted water until soft, and pass through a coarse sieve. Pile the "grains" thus formed on a platter, top with whipped cream and serve.

Omelette Soufflé

INGREDIENTS:
3 egg yolks
3 egg whites
80g flour
50g sugar
Jam
Sifted sugar

METHOD:
Beat butter, sugar and egg yolks until fluffy. Add flour and gently fold in the whisked egg whites. Pour the batter on to a greased round baking tin (rather flat) and bake for some minutes in the oven until the omelette gets a fine light crust. Put on to a platter, spread half of the omelette with jam, fold up the other half and sprinkle with sifted sugar.

Äpfel im Schlafrock
(Apples in their dressing gowns)

INGREDIENTS:
250g flour
150g butter
1 egg yolk
Pinch of salt
2 tablespoons vinegar
3 tablespoons lukewarm water
50g almonds

INGREDIENTS for the filling:
8 apples
⅛l. (approx. 4 fl. ozs) water
40g sugar
60g cranberry jam

METHOD:
Work flour, egg yolk, salt, vinegar and water into a dough, leave to stand for 15 minutes and roll out. Place the butter in the centre, fold the dough over from all sides and roll out and fold again. Repeat this 2 or 3 times. Allow to stand in a cool place for another 15 minutes, then roll out and fold up several times again. Finally roll out and cut the dough into squares big enough to encircle an apple.

Peel the apples and core carefully with a corer. (The apple must remain whole). Bring water and sugar to the boil, add the apples, simmer briefly, drain and leave to cool. Fill the hole in the centre of each apple with cranberry jam.

Place the apples in the dough squares, fold over the four corners and fasten with almonds cut into fine strips. Brush over with the beaten egg yolk, place the apples, suitably attired in their dressing gowns, on a moistened baking tin, and sprinkle with ground almonds. Bake in a hot oven until golden brown.

Nusstorte Tobisch
This is a recipe which has been passed from mother to daughter in a Viennese family for upwards of a hundred years.

Nusstorte Tobisch
(Nut gateau à la Tobisch)

INGREDIENTS:
10 egg whites
200g butter
200g sugar
200g chocolate
200g walnuts
2 to 3 tablespoons of breadcrumbs
Chocolate icing

METHOD:
Cream butter and sugar until fluffy. Gradually add grated or melted chocolate and the ground walnuts. Then carefully fold in the stiffly whisked egg whites and the breadcrumbs.

Put the mixture into a round cake mould previously greased and floured. Bake in a medium oven for about 45 minutes. When cold, invert onto a platter and cover with chocolate icing.

CHAPTER THREE
THE HEURIGER
A 2000-YEAR-OLD CUSTOM

The literal translation of *Heuriger* means *wine of this year*, that is, wine from the last vintage. After Martinmas of the following year *the Heuriger* becomes an *old* wine and ceases to be traded under that name.

For a foreigner *the Heuriger* can be one of the biggest tourist attractions. For an Austrian it means a world in itself. Of course you can export young wine to any country in the world. But is it the same as drinking it in the land of its origin?

What is the magic of *the Heuriger?* Does it lie in the after-sensation of *Gemütlichkeit*, the riot of cheerfulness, accompanied by waltz music and folklore songs, which create that typical Austrian atmosphere? Or is there something much more to it?

Primitive cultures, believing in magic and superstition, do not regard a man's skin as the limit of his being. They assume that the space in which he moves, and the things with which he surrounds himself, are as much part of him as his body. If you allow yourself to be partly overcome by this superstition as you sit under the protecting branches of a huge chestnut tree with a glass of *Heuriger* in front of you, — and all around the enchanting spectacle of endless vineyards wakening to the dawn, — then you have come much closer to the magic circle. Those hours spent between illusion and reality! That is one aspect of the *Heuriger*.

But it can also mean a cheerful picnic on a bright Sunday afternoon, spent with family and friends walking up to the vineyard tavern, where the young wine is served along with simple food, — perhaps in a romantic wine cellar where one can converse the time away.

Such a tavern, where a vineyard owner sells his own wine and food, is called *Buschenschank (schank* a taproom) because of the sprig of pine, or the oval straw sign, hung outside the door. This practice came into being because of a special law, under which the wine in a *Buschenschank* must be self-produced by the owner. Small producers thereby have permission to sell their wine in a *Buschenschank* for a maximum of 300 days a year, but since their vinting is generally not adequate enough to sustain sales throughout the period, they tend to close down early. So the sprig of pine, or sign of straw, became the customary method of indicating that the young wine, always refreshing

and fruity, was still available, and that the *Buschenschank* was still in business.

In Austria the total area under vineyards is more than 40,000 hectares. There are four prominent wine-growing regions. The province of Styria (Bundesland), with its vineyards close to the Yugoslavian border, the province of Burgenland near the Hungarian border, and the Viennese vineyards surrounding the capital deliver 40 per cent of the total Austrian production. The remaining sixty per cent is grown in Lower Austria, in the vineyards of the *Weinviertel*, (or wine-quarter), as well as south of Vienna and along the Danube in a celebrated area known as the Wachau.

The Celtic tribes were producing wine in Austria as far back as 500 B.C. The Romans took over the cultivation in their time, and after Rome had withdrawn, the responsibility was assumed by the nobles and the clergy. Around 1400 the first written reports were made of an extensive export trade in wines, and townships as well as private producers grew wealthy. The first laws for selling *the Heuriger* in a *Buschenschank* date back to 1403, but it is known that these popular taverns were already in existence at the advent of the Christian era.

In mediaeval times about three quarters of the inhabitants of a vine-growing region made their living from wine, and since then the position has not greatly changed. Apart from being an important export item and tourist attraction, wine in Austria has always been regarded as a cultural heritage, meaning much more than its potential for mere alcoholic indulgence.

It is no secret that wine tastes different before and after eating. Again of course it depends upon the kind of food consumed, — the two pleasures should compliment each other. So for *the Heuriger* special dishes came into being, usually offered on a huge buffet-table, where guests help themselves, while the wine is served in glass mugs. (Yes, it has to be mugs.)

Together with this you must have appropriate background music, such as the Harry Lime theme in *The Third Man*. The accordion and the zither are amenable to the typical *Heuriger* atmosphere, which, — depending on the season and the weather, — can be created in an orchard, a rose-garden, a wine cellar, a restaurant, or even in your own lounge.

COLD DISHES

One embarks upon a *Heuriger* with the correct table décor, — simple red and white check cloths, candlelight, a buffet-table and glass mugs. One should also plan to enjoy the occasion without haste, — alternately eating, drinking and talking. And when it is over, the guests go home mellow, scarcely wondering why that indefinable condition of congeniality called *Gemütlichkeit* has found its way into the dictionaries of so many other languages.

At a Buschenschank, *(or taproom)*, in the Southern Styrian wine region.

Grammelschmalz *(Gristles in lard)*
Spread black or brown bread with lard and gristles. Top with chopped onion. In Austria this is *highly* popular at the Heuriger.

Altwiener Rindfleischsalat
(Beef salad old Viennese style)

INGREDIENTS:
500g cold beef (either boiled or roasted)
2 hard-boiled eggs
1 chopped onion

INGREDIENTS for the dressing:
2 hard-boiled eggs
6 tablespoons of oil
6 tablespoons vinegar
½ teaspoon pepper
1 teaspoon salt
1 teaspoon English mustard
1 teaspoon sugar
1 crushed clove of garlic

METHOD:
Cut the meat into small strips and add the finely chopped onion. In a separate bowl crush two hard-boiled egg yolks and gradually stir in the oil. Add salt, pepper, sugar, mustard and garlic as well as vinegar. Chop the 2 hard-boiled egg whites very finely and combine them with the dressing.
Pour the dressing over the meat, cut the remaining hard-boiled eggs into eights, top the salad with them and sprinkle with chopped chive.

Geselchte Zunge mit Oberskren
(Smoked ox-tongue with horseradish sauce)

INGREDIENTS:
1 smoked ox-tongue or 2 calf tongues
Grated horseradish
Some breadcrumbs
Pinch of sugar
Whipped cream or sour cream

METHOD:
Boil the ox-tongue in water until tender. Drain, and while still hot, skin the tongue. Leave to cool.
Meanwhile mix grated horseradish with some breadcrumbs and a pinch of sugar. Add either whipped cream or sour cream to taste.
Slice the tongue, arrange on a platter and garnish with pickled gherkins, — the sauce to be served separately.

Heurigenplatte *(Cold cuts Heuriger style)*

Arrange on a wooden platter black or brown bread, butter, slices of boiled smoked pork, roasted pork and different kinds of cheese. Serve with mustard, horseradish and pickled gherkins. (Note: the smoked pork should preferably be cut from the flank, which in Austria is called *Kaiserfleisch*, or Emperor's meat.)

Gefüllte Paprika *(stuffed peppers)* right.
Kaiserfleisch *(cold smoked pork)*
left foreground.

Leberpastete *(Liver paste)*

INGREDIENTS:
250g pork (breast or shoulder butt)
250g liver
1 large onion
10g lard
2 to 3 peppercorns
Salt
Pepper
Marjoram

METHOD:
Boil the meat together with salt and peppercorns until tender. Meanwhile fry the chopped onion in lard, add the finely sliced liver and continue frying until done. Season with marjoram and pepper. Mince meat and liver, including the onion. Knead the mixture until spreadable and, if necessary, add some more spice to taste.

Liptauer *(Cottage cheese Austrian style)*

INGREDIENTS:
125g butter
250g curds
Salt
Pepper
Paprika
Caraway
1 chopped onion
1 or 2 crushed cloves of garlic
1 teaspoon mustard
8 crushed capers
Chopped chive

METHOD:
Cream the butter until fluffy, add the curds and all other ingredients and mix well.

68

Metternichsalat

As a *Heuriger* means *to spend a most pleasant evening*, the following story concerning the wife of Prince Metternich, after whom this recipe is named, is not inappropriate.

Pauline Metternich was not only one of the most beautiful and charming women of her generation, she was also very quick-witted.

When she celebrated her sixtieth birthday, an Austrian diplomat, searching for a compliment, remarked politely: "Your Excellency! Only sixty! That's no age at all."

"Yes, I agree," answered Pauline Metternich, "It is not really old — for a cathedral!"

Metternichsalat *(Salad à la Metternich)*

INGREDIENTS:
Apples
Cooked celery
Boiled or roasted chicken
Mayonnaise
Tomatoes
Mustard
Truffles

METHOD:
Chop or finely slice equal parts of apples and celery, and mix with the same quantity of diced chicken, (previously cooked). Bind with slightly sweetened mayonnaise, and arrange heaped on a platter.

Surround the salad with tomatoes cut into quarters, and garnish in a criss-cross pattern with fine threads of mustard. Finally sprinkle with chopped truffles and serve.

Nudelsalat *(Noodle salad)*

INGREDIENTS:
500g boiled cold noodles
250g roasted cold diced meat (chicken or pork)
1 cucumber
3 tomatoes
3 green peppers

INGREDIENTS for the dressing:
⅛l. (approx. 4 fl. ozs) sour cream
1 yoghurt
Some mayonnaise
Chopped parsley
Powdered curry
Salt
Pepper

METHOD:
Combine the noodles with the diced meat and finely sliced cucumbers, tomatoes and green peppers. Mix all ingredients for the dressing, and pour over the salad. Leave to stand for at least half-an-hour.

Zungensalat *(Ox-tongue salad with potatoes)*

INGREDIENTS:
250g boiled potatoes
250g boiled ox-tongue
1 apple
1 small onion
3 tablespoons of oil
3 tablespoons of vinegar
4-6 tablespoons cold stock
Salt
Pepper

METHOD:
Boil and peel the potatoes. When still warm, cut them into dices about ½ inch square. Add the diced apples, the diced boiled ox-tongue and the finely chopped onion.

Mix oil, vinegar, the spices and cold stock. Pour the dressing over the salad. Allow to stand for at least half-an-hour.

Sulz *(Jellied head of pork — a very popular dish for the Heuriger in Austria)*

INGREDIENTS:
2 feet and 1 pig's head
Root vegetables
Salt
Some peppercorns
1 whole nutmeg
1 bay leaf
Thyme
Wine vinegar
Sliced onion
Some carrots
Sliced pickled gherkins

METHOD:
Boil head and feet of the pig with sliced root vegetables, salt, pepper, nutmeg, bay leaf, thyme and wine vinegar until tender. Drain and remove the meat from the bones while still warm. Dice the meat and mix with the boiled diced carrots, sliced fried onion and sliced pickled gherkins. Put the mixture into the strained soup and allow to jellify in a cool place. Invert on to a platter and cut the *Sulz* into slices. Top each slice with chopped onion, and pour over with a mixture of oil and vinegar.

Grammelschmalzbrot *(gristles in lard, spread on black-bread)* left.
Liptauer *(cottage cheese Austrian style)* right foreground.
Sulz *(jellied head of pork)* right background.

Warm Dishes

In the second half of the last century *the Heuriger* even inspired a special type of music, which still graces the occasion to this day. The Viennese musicians Johann and Josef Schrammel founded a quartet consisting of two violins, 1 guitar and an accordion, and started to play folk and dancing music in the taverns. Soon their particular style and orchestration became associated with *the Heuriger* and was generally known as *Schrammel-musik*.

A hundred years earlier, another musician, Christoph Willibald Gluck, who spent half of his life in Vienna, and had come to enjoy *the Heuriger,* — once gave it high recognition when he declared that the three things he wished most were "money, wine and fame". When asked why fame seemed to rate lowest of these three, he said, "With money I buy wine, the wine creates inspiration, and from inspiration fame must surely follow."

Backhendl

Out of all the ways of preparing chicken in Austria, the *Backhendl* (chicken with a coating like the Wiener Schnitzel) is the most popular. By 1800 the *Backhendl* had become inseparably associated with the Vienna *Prater* – or amusement park – long before the Giant Wheel was erected there. The two restaurants offering this particular dish in the *Prater* were said to have sold 440,000 chickens in a year, this at a time when the entire population of Vienna was no more than 360,000. From the Prater the *Backhendl* soon spread in triumph to *the Heuriger* taverns around Vienna, where it is still the favourite today.

Backhendl *(Fried chicken)*

INGREDIENTS:
Per person ½ chicken
Pinch of salt
2 eggs
Flour and breadcrumbs for the coating
Cooking fat

METHOD:
Divide the young chicken into four pieces, roll each piece in flour, dip into beaten eggs and coat with breadcrumbs, shaking off the excess. Fry in deep hot cooking fat until crisp and golden brown. Drain on a wire rack and garnish with lemon slices and parsley. Serve with lettuce or a green mixed salad.

Bratwürstel mit Senfsauce
(Fried sausages with mustard sauce)

INGREDIENTS for the sausages:
250g minced pork
100g streaky bacon
¹⁄₁₆l. (approx. 2fl.ozs) water
1 chopped onion
1 crushed clove of garlic
Pepper
Salt
Powdered ginger
Marjoram

METHOD:
    Combine the minced pork with the finely diced or chopped bacon, and add chopped onion, crushed garlic and the spices. Then stir in water drop by drop and knead the meat into a smooth paste. Form small cylinders 2½ to 3 inches long, dip each one into flour and fry in hot cooking fat.
    Serve with white bread or toast and cold mustard sauce.

INGREDIENTS for the mustard sauce:
4 hard-boiled eggs
3 anchovies
2 tablespoons of chopped parsley
Mustard
Pinch of sugar
Wine vinegar mixed with water

METHOD:
    Chop the hard-boiled eggs and anchovies very finely, or put them together with the wine vinegar into the blender to get a pulp.
    Add finely chopped parsley, mustard to taste and a pinch of salt. Stir well until you get a thick sauce.

Gebratene Stelze *(Roasted knuckle of veal or pork)*

INGREDIENTS:
1 knuckle of veal or pork
Salt
Pepper
Crushed garlic
¼ to ½l. (approx. 9 to 18 fl.ozs) stock
Oil and butter as required

METHOD:
    Combine salt, pepper and crushed garlic with some oil. Rub the knuckle of veal with the mixture, and allow to stand overnight. Then fry on all sides briefly in hot butter to colour it. Remove from heat. Put some stock in a roasting tin, add the meat, cover and roast gently – depending on the size of the knuckle, this could take several hours. (To test for readiness prick with a fork and watch for a clear drop of liquid springing out.)
    While roasting, baste frequently and add more stock if necessary. When the knuckle is almost cooked, remove the cover and continue roasting in a very hot oven until golden brown. Serve with rice and lettuce.

Kalbsburger Schweinsripperl
(Spare ribs Kalbsburg style)

INGREDIENTS:
800g spare ribs (pork)
1 onion
2 pieces castor sugar
4 cooking apples
1kg sauerkraut
Lard
1 clove garlic
1 teaspoon paprika
Salt
Caraway
Thyme
1 bay leaf

METHOD:
    Rub the spare ribs with a mixture of salt, paprika, caraway and crushed garlic. Fry them briefly in hot lard on all sides, remove from heat and put aside.
    In the same lard fry the chopped onion together with the castor sugar. Add the cored and sliced apples, the sauerkraut, salt, thyme, bay leaf and stock. Put the spare ribs on top and simmer until soft.

Fleischlaiberl mit Gurkensauce
(Minced meat with cucumber sauce)

INGREDIENTS:
250g minced meat
1 stale roll
1 onion
1 or 2 crushed garlic cloves
50g butter
2 eggs
Marjoram
Salt
Pepper
2 tablespoons sour cream
2 tablespoons breadcrumbs
Cooking fat

METHOD:
Mix the minced meat with the roll moistened in milk and squeezed. Add chopped onion, crushed garlic, salt, pepper and marjoram. In a separate bowl cream butter until fluffy. Gradually stir in the beaten eggs. Add this to the minced meat. Finally stir in the sour cream and breadcrumbs. Knead well, then form into balls of about 2 inches diameter. Press each ball flat until it becomes approximately 1 inch thick.

Fry in hot cooking fat on each side, and serve with either bread or potatoes and cucumber sauce.

INGREDIENTS for the cucumber sauce:
1 cucumber
1 onion
50g butter
¼l. (approx. 9 fl. ozs) stock
1 tablespoon flour
Chopped parsley
1 tablespoon sour cream
Salt
Pepper

METHOD:
Peel the cucumber and cut horizontally into halves. Core and dice. Heat butter and fry the chopped onion and the finely diced cucumber until soft. Dust with flour, and gradually stir in the cold stock. Bring to the boil and simmer for about 3 minutes. Season with salt, pepper, and chopped parsley. Finally stir in the sour cream.

Fleischlaiberl *(minced meat)* left, smoked, boiled pork chops right. Kartoffelkäs *(potato-cheese)* background.

Krautstrudel

It is an indication of the reverence once bestowed in Austria upon the *strudel*, — cabbage-filled for *the Heuriger*, — that in the 18th century a fiancé would test his prospective bride's culinary prowess on just such a delicacy.

The most notorious example was Karl Stellwag, a renowned oculist and professor at Vienna University. For decades the doctor had stayed a bachelor, utterly spoiled by a Bohemian cooking maid, who looked after all his needs, and made the most wonderful *strudel*. But one day fate dealt him a harsh blow. The maid became engaged to a policeman and promptly handed in her notice. This was too much for him to bear, so he tore up the notice, and married her himself.

Krautstrudel *(Cabbage strudel)*

INGREDIENTS for the dough:
200g flour
Pinch of salt
1 tablespoon oil
Lukewarm water as required
    (approx. 3 tablespoons)

INGREDIENTS for the filling:
500 to 600g chopped white cabbage
250 to 300g chopped ham or bacon
1 chopped onion
30g butter
Salt
Pepper
Caraway
100g breadcrumbs fried in 80g butter

METHOD:
Work the ingredients for the dough together in the same way as for *Apfelstrudel* (see chapter 1).

Fry the chopped onion in butter. Add the chopped cabbage and season with salt, pepper and caraway. Cook until the cabbage is tender but still crisp and not too soft. Stir in the ham and allow to cool.

Meanwhile roll out the dough on a floured cloth until very thin. Sprinkle two-thirds with breadcrumbs fried in butter, and cover with the cabbage mixture. Roll the dough up firmly, ending with the third still uncovered. Place the *strudel* on a greased baking tin and brush over with softened butter. Bake in a rather hot oven until golden brown. Serve hot.

Krenfleisch *(Boiled pork with horseradish)*

INGREDIENTS:
1½kg pork (cut from the flank)
¼l. (approx. 9 fl. ozs) vinegar
Some peppercorns
1 carrot
¼ celery root
½ parsley root
½ onion
150g grated horseradish
Salt
Caraway
1 bay leaf
Pickled gherkins, grated horseradish
    and mustard for garnishing.

METHOD:

Put the meat in a pot together with the roughly chopped root-vegetables, vinegar, peppercorns, onion, grated horseradish, bay leaf and caraway. Pour over with boiling salted water, and boil until the meat is tender, but not too soft. Drain, and cut the meat into slices. Serve with pickled gherkins, mustard and grated horseradish together with brown and black bread.

Reisfleisch *(Pilaff)*

INGREDIENTS:
½kg pork (cut from the shoulder)
50g margarine
1 large onion
2 tablespoons paprika
1 crushed clove of garlic
1 cup rice
3 cups of stock
Pinch of salt
Caraway
Marjoram
Grated Parmesan cheese

METHOD:
Fry the chopped onion in margarine and add the meat, cut as finely as possible. Season with salt, paprika, caraway, garlic and marjoram. Fry until half tender. Add the rice and stock. Bring to the boil and stew gently until the rice is cooked and dry. Sprinkle generously with Parmesan cheese and serve with lettuce or a green mixed salad.

Kartoffelkäs *(Potato cheese)*
Mix boiled and sliced potatoes with plenty of finely chopped onion, salt, pepper and sour cream. Serve separately with the sausages.

Überbackene Schinkenfleckerl
(Fried noodles with ham)

INGREDIENTS *for the noodle dough:*
200g flour
1 egg
Pinch of salt
Lukewarm water as required

INGREDIENTS *for the filling:*
100g butter
2 egg yolks
2 egg whites
300g minced ham
Pinch of salt
⅛l. (approx. 4 fl. ozs) sour cream

METHOD:
Work all ingredients for the dough together, knead well and roll out to about ⅛ inch thickness. Cut into ½inch squares. Boil the squares in salted water, drain and set aside.

Beat butter until fluffy, add egg yolks, pinch of salt, the minced ham, sour cream and the boiled dough-squares. Finally fold in the stiffly whisked egg whites. Spread a baking tin with butter, sprinkle with breadcrumbs and fill the mixture into it. Bake for about half to three quarters of an hour until golden brown. Serve with lettuce.

Schinkenwürfel mit Kartoffelkäs
(Ham sausages with potato cheese)

INGREDIENTS:
50g butter
50g flour
⅛l. (approx. 4 fl. ozs) milk
500g boiled smoked pork or ham
2 egg yolks
Sour cream as required
Flour
1 or 2 eggs
Breadcrumbs for coating
Cooking fat

METHOD:
Heat butter and stir in flour. Gradually add cold milk until you get a smooth thick sauce. Leave to get cold. Add egg yolks, the minced ham or smoked pork, pinch of salt, and sufficient sour cream to get a smooth paste.

Form cylinders about 3 inches long, roll each cylinder in flour, dip into beaten eggs and coat with breadcrumbs. Fry in hot deep cooking fat until golden brown.

DINING WITH
RICHARD THE LIONHEART

Probably the first Briton to savour Austrian dishes cooked in their native environment was Richard Coeur de Lion, captured on his way back from the Third Crusade by Duke Leopold V of Austria, who held a grudge against him for a previous offence, and imprisoned him in the Castle of Dürnstein, now a tourist attraction.

This was in 1192 A.D., and according to legend, Richard's singer Blondel managed to find the castle and free him. However, what really happened was that the English had to pay a ransom of 35,000 pounds of silver for the return of their king, and from the proceeds a city was built, thus linking King Richard into Austrian history, which may be said to have started in that region, later known as the *Wachau*. It grew to what is now the province of Lower Austria (Niederösterreich), and was first mentioned in the history books of 966 as *regio osttarrichi*.

Dating back to earliest times, there were trade routes crossing Lower Austria from the North Sea, from the Adriatic and from the north-east via the Moravian gate, — as well as the pre-historic *amber* trail. Illyric, Celtic and Germanic tribes, Romans and Slavs settled there, and their own traditions became interwoven with those already existing in the country. Later, through numerous wars, Huns, Turks, Magyars, Swedes and Frenchmen invaded the region, leaving their mark in more ways than one. Their national habits of preparing food became absorbed into the culture of the area, resulting in a wealth of delicious if less than exotic dishes,– what one might call the culinary souvenir of a millennium.

A journey through the Wachau today still shows what this millennium must have been like. Surrounded by sunny vineyards and hundreds of apricot trees, almost every village is a separate experience. What you see is at least a hundred years old, but more likely four hundred or five hundred years. These villages, strung like pearls on a string along the banks of the Danube, tell their own stories, with their dreamy courtyards, shady arcades and the avalanches of roses which create a timeless atmosphere full of peace.

Here and there lie numerous castle ruins; former strongholds of robber barons who stretched chains across the river so that every passing vessel would be obliged to pay them a fee; or perhaps the remains of mighty monasteries, which had once

cultivated the whole area. The Danube itself, like a silver ribbon, seems not only to connect country to country, but generation to generation. And further north, in the *Waldviertel* amongst endless forests one can find scattered ponds and hidden castles, full of quiet beauty, which seem to belong to another era. It is an area where life has not changed much through the centuries.

Folk-music in the Waldviertel.

Nearly 60 per cent of the land in Lower Austria is used for agriculture or the vine, whilst a third is still afforested. A farmer's life in the Waldviertel is by no means easy. But in the evenings folk music and folk dances are practised, as the bustling housewives work on their traditional dishes. It might be soups and stews, pork or possibly mutton, mainly prepared along with the plentiful potato; dumplings in their many variations; poppy seed noodles and desserts fried in lard. In former times beef and veal were reserved for special occasions only. The reason for this was that pigs were fed for slaughtering, while cows were kept for their milk and hens for their eggs. Potatoes, vegetables and fruits were grown in the garden, and very little was brought in from outside. Yet what an incredible number of dishes were created from those simple resources!

The nobility and the monasteries held the fishing and hunting rights between them, which meant that fish and venison were delicacies seldom seen by the lower orders. Therefore it took rather a long time for dishes of that nature to become established amongst the farmers and the middle classes, though carp was traditionally served on Christmas Eve, and venison is now a speciality of the region.

The Wachau's reputation as a wine-growing region reaches back to the Middle Ages. In the 14th century for instance the small township of Krems/Stein exported no less than 300,000 gallons of wine annually. In modern times it is not only the high quality of the wine, but also the beauty of the region, combined with its proximity to Vienna, which attracts visitors, who then are eager to try out the local and regional dishes.

Because a *genuine* dish cannot be invented like a cocktail, old and trusted recipes are treasured, being passed from mother to daughter in private notebooks. The first official recipe collection was published in 1683 by the baroque poet Wolf Helmhard von Hoberg. 100 years later a second cookery book was printed, which finally became the basis of a more extended one, written by the cook to Prince Schwarzenberg, who emphasised in his preface that all 1130 recipes were to be accepted as *genuine* dishes of Lower Austria.

Subsequently, of course, more and more books became available, containing not only regional dishes, but also recipes from the whole of

The Renaissance castle of Schallaburg in the Wachau.

Austria. No doubt these were subject to alteration as certain ingredients grew scarce in times of war and privation.

However, many of the *genuine* regional recipes still date back either to Prince Schwarzenberg's cook, or to that family secret passed between mother and daughter. So many distinguished visitors to the Wachau, along with thousands of ordinary tourists, have taken home with them not only the memory of a lovely area, but also the substantial pleasure of having enjoyed a baroque meal which, armed with the appropriate recipes, can be reproduced for them at any time or place.

Balancing rocks typical of the Waldviertel.

SOUPS & STEWS

In Austria, it is sometimes difficult to differentiate between a soup and a stew, but the popular thick soups had several origins. Many varieties were brought from Hungary as goulashes, from Serbia as with bean soup, and potato soup from Bohemia. At the same time it was a traditional farmer's dish in the countryside, being served for breakfast as well as lunch or supper. Up to the Napoleonic era the nobility and middle class preferred clear soup. But when the French army swept through the country and the Austrians saw Napoleon eating *pot au feu*, (the French thick soup), thick soups became acceptable in the capital.

CLEAR SOUPS

Backerbsensuppe *("Pea" soup)*

INGREDIENTS:
1 cup milk
1 egg
Pinch of salt
Flour as required
Lard for frying
Beef broth

METHOD:
Mix milk, salt and the beaten egg together and add as much flour as needed to get a smooth batter. Heat lard in a pan until very hot. By using a coarse grater, held bottom side up, allow the batter to drip into the hot fat. Fry the pea-sized lumps until golden brown. Drain and serve separately with the beef broth. Before the meal starts put 1 to 2 tablespoons of fried "peas" into each soup plate, then pour in the hot beef broth.

Junggesellensuppe *(Bachelor's soup)*

INGREDIENTS:
2 stale rolls or white bread
3 eggs
1 tablespoon milk or cream
Cooking fat
Beef broth or stock

METHOD:
Mix milk or cream with the beaten eggs and pour this over the diced rolls. Allow to soak until the liquid is absorbed completely. Heat cooking fat in a pan and fry the diced bread until golden brown. Pour in hot beef broth or stock and serve immediately.

Chinesenzopf *(Chinese plait)*

INGREDIENTS:
50g butter
2 eggs
1 bread roll moistened in milk and squeezed
40g ham
40g leftovers of roasted meat
40g diced carrots
40g green peas
Salt
Pepper
Sour cream as required
Beef broth

METHOD:
Beat butter and the whole eggs until fluffy. Stir in the squeezed roll. By and by add the finely diced ham, meat, carrots, peas and sour cream as required to get a medium firm dough. Season with pepper and salt. Work the dough into a cylinder of 2 inches diameter. Roll the cylinder firmly in a butter-spread kitchen cloth and boil in salted water for about one hour. Leave to cool, cut into slices and serve in a hot beef broth.

THICK SOUPS

Panadelsuppe *(White bread soup)*

INGREDIENTS:
2 rolls
60g butter
1 chopped onion
Chopped parsley
Salt
Pepper
¾l. (approx. 26 fl.ozs) stock
1 egg yolk

METHOD:
Fry the chopped onion and parsley in butter, add the rolls cut into neat pieces, and pour on the cold stock. Bring to the boil and simmer for about 15 minutes. Remove from heat, pass the soup through a sieve and season with salt and pepper. Heat up again and stir in the egg yolk without boiling.

Brotsuppe *(Black bread soup)*

INGREDIENTS:
2 or 3 large slices of brown or black bread
Cooking fat
1 egg yolk
3 tablespoons of sour cream
1 fincly sliced sausage per person
Chopped chive
Salt
Pepper
Caraway
1 crushed clove of garlic
1l. (approx. 35fl.ozs) stock

METHOD:
Cut the bread into small pieces and fry in hot cooking fat without browning. Add salt, pepper, caraway and garlic. Pour in the stock and cook for about 15 minutes. Before serving, add the egg yolk, the sour cream and the sliced sausages. Bring to the boil and serve with plenty of chopped chive.

Böhmische Suppe *(Bohemian soup)*

INGREDIENTS:
1 small head of shredded white cabbage
Some mushrooms
50g butter
50g streaky bacon
2 level teaspoons flour
Salt
Pepper
Caraway
1l. (approx. 35fl.ozs) stock

METHOD:
Heat butter, add the shredded cabbage and finely sliced mushrooms. Mix well, then pour in most of the stock. Season with salt, pepper, caraway. Simmer until the cabbage is soft. If the stock gets too much reduced, add some more.
Meanwhile fry the finely diced bacon and drain off. Dust the soup with flour, bring to the boil again, add the fried bacon and serve with white bread.

Gerstensuppe à la Madelaine
(Pearl barley soup, an old family recipe)

INGREDIENTS:
100g pearl barley
100g streaky bacon
Stock as required
20g flour
1 egg yolk
2 to 3 tablespoons cream

METHOD:
Boil the pearl barley by always pouring in sufficient stock to cover until soft (approximately 2 hours).
Meanwhile fry the finely diced bacon in a separate pan until crisp, drain and add to the soup. Stir 20g flour into the remaining lard in the pan and pour over with water to get a smooth paste. Remove from heat, add the egg yolk and 2 to 3 tablespoons of cream. Add this mixture to the soup, bring to the boil once more and serve.

Waldviertler Linsensuppe
(Lentil soup Waldviertel style)

INGREDIENTS:
150g lentils
1 bay leaf
Thyme
Pepper
1 slice of lemon
50g pearl barley
1 onion
40g cooking fat
60g streaky bacon
150g liver
200g carrots
1 tablespoon flour
4 tablespoons buttermilk
1 tablespoon mustard
2 tablespoons tomato purée
1 tablespoon vinegar
Chopped chive

METHOD:
   Soak lentils and pearl barley in water overnight, and drain. Boil lentils and pearl barley together with salt, pepper, bay leaf, thyme and a slice of lemon in water, until medium to soft.

   Heat cooking fat in a separate pan and fry the finely diced bacon and chopped onion without browning. Add the diced liver and the diced carrots and continue frying for some minutes. Remove from heat, add to the soup and cook until the lentils almost fall into pieces. Mix butter, milk, flour, mustard and tomato purée. Stir this mixture into the soup. Add vinegar with plenty of chopped chive, and serve.

STEWS

Serbische Bohnensuppe

In former times beans and peas were considered to have occult powers. So, for instance, bean soup was cooked on the second of November (Holy Souls), and on the 24th December. According to the legend those who do not eat bean soup on Christmas Eve will become donkeys.

Peas were considered a symbol of fertility, and were served at Easter, on the 24th of June and every Thursday. At a wedding raw peas were poured over the bride, – as is still done with rice in India.

Serbische Bohnensuppe *(Serbian bean soup)*

INGREDIENTS:
200g smoked pork
**   (preferably cut from the flank)**
2 small onions
20g paprika
1 tablespoon tomato purée
200g previously cooked or tinned white beans
1 bay leaf
1 clove crushed garlic
Salt
Vinegar to taste
Stock as required

METHOD:
Fry the chopped onion and finely diced meat in cooking fat. Add the spices, tomato purée and some vinegar. Pour in stock to cover, and simmer until the meat is soft. Add the beans, dust with some flour and stir in as much stock as required, — depending on whether you want a soup or a stew. Continue cooking for some more minutes and serve.

Erdäpfelgulasch *(Potato goulash)*

INGREDIENTS:
750g potatoes
250g onion
250g sausages
Stock as required
Salt
Pepper
Caraway
Paprika
1 or 2 crushed cloves garlic

METHOD:
Fry the chopped onion in hot cooking fat. Add the spices and the peeled and diced potatoes. Fry for some minutes, stirring constantly. Pour in sufficient stock to cover, and simmer until the potatoes are soft. Before serving, add the finely sliced sausages, bring to the boil and serve.

STARTERS & SNACKS

Eierwürstel *(Roasted pancake)*

INGREDIENTS for the pancake:
250g flour
1 egg
Pinch of salt
½l. (approx. 18fl.ozs) milk
Cooking fat

INGREDIENTS for the filling:
30g butter
1 egg
3 hard-boiled eggs
Chopped parsley
Salt
Pepper
Sour cream
½ roll moistened in milk and squeezed

METHOD:
Mix all ingredients for the pancakes into a smooth batter. Heat cooking fat and fry – one at a time – approximately 10 pancakes. Put aside and keep warm.

Cream butter and egg until fluffy. Add the finely chopped hard-boiled eggs, the chopped parsley, salt, pepper, and the squeezed bread roll. Mix well and add as much sour cream as needed to get a smooth paste.

Spread each pancake with the mixture and roll up firmly. Grease a baking tin and pour in as much sour cream as needed to cover the bottom. Fit the pancakes one after the other into the tin, top with sour cream and bake in a medium oven until the cream gets slightly yellow.

Lutherische Eier *(Eggs Luther style)*

INGREDIENTS:
6 eggs
Pepper
Salt
1 tablespoon chopped onion
Chopped parsley
100g ham
6 medium sized mushrooms
Butter

METHOD:
Fry the chopped onion in butter, then add parsley, sliced mushrooms and the ham cut into strips. Fry until the mushrooms get soft, and leave to cool.

Beat the eggs and season with salt and pepper. Stir in the cold ham and mushroom mixture. Heat butter in an omelette pan, pour the mixture on to it and fry on both sides until golden brown. Cut into squares and serve with lettuce.

The extensive woods in the Waldviertel, with their numerous ponds, have always provided enough fowl and fish, — which, as noted, were formerly the preserve of the monks and the nobility, to whom they provided many a favourite dish.

From the impressive Cistercian monastery at Zwettl, the whole region was brought under cultivation. Today the monastery is still a cultural centre. Its beautiful Gothic cross-gallery has often been used as background in international films, including one featuring the Austrian-born Romy Schneider.

The region still observes its traditional feudal days, and castles with their surrounding manorial woods dominate the scene.

One of the countless small ponds glittering between far-stretching forests.

Fasan in Kraut *(Pheasant with white cabbage)*

INGREDIENTS:

1 pheasant
50g bacon
Cooking fat
Salt
Pepper
1 head of white cabbage
30g butter
1 onion
1 tablespoon sugar
Vinegar to taste

METHOD:

Prepare the pheasant and rub inside with salt and pepper.

Cut the bacon into thin slices, place them on the breast and fry the pheasant briefly in hot cooking fat on all sides. Put aside.

Heat butter, add sugar and fry until slightly brown. Stir in the finely chopped onion and the shredded cabbage. Pour over some water mixed with vinegar and continue cooking for some minutes. Then add the pheasant and simmer until tender.

Gebratene Wachteln *(Roast quail)*

INGREDIENTS:

6 quails
150g bacon
70g butter
Pepper
Salt
Stock
¼l. (approx. 9fl.ozs) sour cream

METHOD:

Prepare and wash the quail. Rub inside and outside with pepper and salt. Wrap in rashers of bacon. Put butter in a roasting tin, add some water or stock and arrange the quails within. Roast approximately ¾ hour, basting now and then, adding some stock if necessary. When almost cooked, pour in the sour cream mixed with a teaspoon of flour, and continue roasting for some minutes. Serve with stewed cranberries and boiled rice.

Karpfen in Rotwein *(Carp in red wine)*

INGREDIENTS:
1 carp
⅜l. (approx. 13fl.ozs) red wine
⅛l. (approx. 4fl.ozs) wine vinegar
1 onion
6 peppercorns
6 cloves
Salt

METHOD:
Gut and clean the carp, cut into portions and salt. Put a mixture of red wine and wine vinegar in a casserole, add the onion cut into halves, the peppercorns and the cloves, and bring to the boil. Then add the pieces of the carp and simmer until cooked. Put the fish pieces on a platter and keep warm. Continue cooking the sauce until half reduced, pass through a sieve and pour over the carp.

Lembraten *(Fried kidneys Austrian style)*

INGREDIENTS:
1 calf's kidney,
1 onion
Cooking fat
Chopped parsley
Salt
Marjoram
Pepper
Paprika
1 level teaspoon flour
1 teaspoon vinegar
1 teaspoon mustard
Water

METHOD:
Skin and clean the kidney. Fry the chopped onion and parsley in hot cooking fat, add the sliced kidney and continue frying, stirring regularly until cooked. Dust with flour. Add some water or stock and season with salt, pepper, marjoram, paprika, mustard and vinegar. Bring to the boil, cook for some minutes and serve.

Rindszunge in Sardellensauce
(Ox-tongue with anchovy sauce)

INGREDIENTS:
1 ox tongue
1 level teaspoon anchovy paste
70 to 80g butter
Breadcrumbs
⅛l. (approx. 4 fl. ozs) sour cream

METHOD:
Put the ox-tongue into salted water and simmer until tender. Drain, and while still hot, skin the tongue. Cut into slices approx. half-an-inch thick and put aside.

Mix butter with anchovy paste and spread each side of the tongue slices with the mixture. Fit the slices, closely and slightly overlapping, into a rather flat ovenware dish or roasting tin. Sprinkle generously with breadcrumbs and pour over with sour cream. Bake until the sour cream gets slightly yellow, and serve with boiled potatoes.

Goulash

This Hungarian dish was originally cooked in a huge kettle by the herdsmen of the *Puszta* or Great Plain of Hungary. From there it made its way to Austria, where it might appear as a main dish, but is much more popular as a snack, served with only a roll and an obligatory glass of beer.

Austrian menus always offer a huge variety of goulashes: *Fiaker-Gulasch*, served with a Viennese sausage, a hard-boiled egg and pickled gherkins; the *Sacher-Gulasch* with pickled gherkins and pommes frites; or the *Szegediner* with sauerkraut, to name just a few of them.

The meat used for the goulash can be beef, calf or pork, or like the *Husarengulasch*, consist of all three kinds. (Beef then has to be cooked longer). But the main secret for any kind of goulash is always to take as much onion as meat, — then your dish will be a success. (The only exception to this is the *Szegediner Gulasch*).

With due regard for its outdoor origins, a garden party is a good occasion to experiment with goulash, boiling it in a kettle on an open fire. Try your own *Puszta* night with Czardas music in the background.

Gulasch mit Nockerl
(Goulash and flour dumplings).
Wachauer Marillenknödel
(apricot dumplings à la Wachau)
right background.

Gulasch *(Goulash)*

INGREDIENTS:
600g diced meat (beef, calf or pork)
600g finely chopped onions
100g cooking fat
2 tablespoons paprika
Salt
Caraway
1 or 2 crushed cloves garlic
Stock

METHOD:
Fry the finely chopped onion in cooking fat without browning. Add the spices and the meat. Gradually pour on sufficient stock to cover the meat, bring to the boil and simmer until the meat is tender. The gravy when served must not be too thin. As a snack, serve with a roll, as a main dish with either boiled potatoes or *Nockerl* (see page 53).

Szegediner Krautfleisch or Szegediner Gulasch
(Pork and sauerkraut à la Szegedin)

INGREDIENTS:
600g shoulder of pork
40g oil
150g onion
20g paprika
Salt
Caraway
1 crushed clove of garlic
Stock
500g sauerkraut
1 raw grated potato

METHOD:
Fry the chopped onion in oil and add the diced meat. Continue frying for some minutes in order to colour the meat, season with salt, caraway, paprika and garlic, and moisten with some stock. Cover and stew gently until the meat is half-done. Add sauerkraut, and if necessary, some more stock. Continue stewing until the meat is soft, then congeal with grated raw potato.

Serve with boilded potatoes.

Topfenhaluska *(Noodles with bacon and curds)*

INGREDIENTS for the dough:
200g flour
2 eggs
Lukewarm water as required

INGREDIENTS for the filling:
150g finely diced streaky bacon
150g strained curds
Pinch of salt

METHOD:
Place the flour on a board, make a hole in the centre and break the eggs into it. Working from the middle outwards and adding as much water as required, knead into a rather firm dough. Leave to stand for a while, then divide into four parts. Roll each part out as thin as possible (one at a time) and cut into squares. Cook in salted water and drain.

Fry the diced bacon slowly until you get gristles. Remove the gristles and put the dough squares into the hot fat. Mix well, place in a bowl and stir in the curds and the gristles.

MAIN DISHES

The monastery of Melk, famous for its library.

B<u>EE</u>F

One of the occasions for which beef dishes were reserved in former days was a pilgrimage.

Pilgrimage churches are common in Austria, and since it is a 97 per cent Catholic country, most of them are devoted to *Our Lady*. Generally, too, they came into being because of some miracle which had happened on that certain spot, so that the faithful had felt impelled to build a church in commemoration.

An exception to this is the Maria Laach, a pilgrimage church on the road leading from the Wachau to the Waldviertel. A side altar picture in this church attracted attention because of a 15th century artist who perpetrated a whimsical joke, in which he depicted Our Lady with six fingers on one hand. Inevitably it came to be called *The Church to Our Lady with Six Fingers*, and starting as a curiosity, the place became a resort for pilgrims drawn to this unusual spectacle.

Mostbraten *(Beef in cider sauce)*

INGREDIENTS:
100 to 150g bacon
40g cooking fat
50g carrots
50g parsley roots
50g onion
1kg beef (rump or fillet)
4 cloves
1 small piece ginger
1 tablespoon vinegar
Cider and water mixed (half and half)
Salt
Pepper
3 level teaspoons flour

METHOD:
Put the oil in a high-sided roasting pan and cover the bottom evenly with rashers of bacon. Top up with the finely cut root vegetables and chopped onion.

Rub the meat with salt and pepper, place in the roasting pan and add ginger and cloves. Mix water, cider and vinegar, and pour over the meat until the pan is one third full. Cover and roast in the oven until the meat is cooked, basting now and then.

When soft, remove the meat and keep warm. Dust the gravy with flour, and simmer for a while until you get a thickish sauce. (If too thick, add some more water-cider mixture).

Season with salt and pepper, pass through a sieve and pour over the sliced meat. Serve with raw potato dumplings. (See *Hauerknödel,* side dishes page 101).

PORK

In the Wachau region feast days come as a welcome relaxation after the hard work in the vineyards. One of the most picturesque is the *Johannisnacht*, held on the eve of 23rd June, commemorating the birth of John the Baptist.

A myriad of torches illuminate *Thousand-bucket-mountain* at the village of Spitz, — so named because 1000 buckets of grapes are annually cropped there. Meanwhile everyone dresses up in traditional costume, the women's caps being especially remarkable and precious. The night is then celebrated in the vineyards and the taverns.

Roast pork, even more popular in the countryside than Wiener Schnitzel, is absolutely obligatory on such occasions. (It is by the way also the traditional New Year's dish). For the Teutonic tribes the pig has always been a symbol of luck, strength and fertility, and was probably cooked in that region long before Christ.

Another symbol of fertility, a small statue of clay called the *Venus of Willendorf*, shows the Wachau was inhabited in prehistoric times. The statue was discovered by accident some decades ago, and is calculated to be about 25,000 years old.

Böhmisches Bierfleisch
(Pork in beer Bohemian style)

INGREDIENTS:
1kg shoulder of pork
Salt
Pepper
Caraway
Beer as required
3 to 4 tablespoons breadcrumbs
   (from brown or black bread)

METHOD:
Cut the meat into dices about 1 inch square. Season with salt, pepper and caraway. Simmer in beer until the meat is tender. Before removing from heat, add breadcrumbs and continue cooking gently for about ten minutes. Serve with Bohemian dumplings. (See *Böhmische Knödel*, side dishes page 99).

Böhmisches Bierfleisch *(pork in beer)*
left foreground.
Böhmische Knödel *(Bohemian dumplings)*
right.
Waldviertler Mohnnudeln
(potato noodles with poppy seed)
background.

Schweinsbraten *(Roast pork)*

INGREDIENTS:
1 kg pork
Salt
Pepper
Caraway
1 to 2 cloves of garlic
Margarine
Some stock

METHOD:
Rub the meat with salt, pepper and crushed garlic, and sprinkle generously with caraway. Leave to stand overnight. Heat margarine in a roasting pan and colour the meat briefly on all sides. Add 2 to 3 tablespoons of stock and put into the oven. Roast gently without covering until the meat gets crisp, basting frequently. Add more stock if necessary, but there must never be too much liquid in the pan. When crisp upside, turn the meat over until the other side crisps as well. When cooked, put the meat on a platter, dust the gravy with some flour and pour over. Serve with cabbage dumplings. (See *Krautknödel*, page 100).

Schweinsbraten *(roast pork)* and Waldviertler Knödel *(dumplings Waldviertel style)*, Krautsalat mit Speck *(warm cabbage salad with bacon)* left background.

Waldviertler Jungschweinbraten
(Pork Waldviertel style)

INGREDIENTS:
1 kg pork
⅛ l. (approx. 4 fl. ozs) stock
⅛ l. (approx. 4 fl. ozs) white wine
1 level tablespoon caraway
1 onion
1 apple
2 cloves garlic
1 bay leaf
Salt
Thyme

METHOD:
Crush the garlic, mix with salt and caraway, and rub the meat with this mixture. Place the meat in a roasting pan, add the finely chopped onion, the cored and roughly sliced apples, bay leaf and thyme.

Pour in the stock, cover and roast in a medium oven until the meat is almost tender, basting now and then. Pour over the white wine, and continue roasting uncovered for about ten minutes in a hot oven to get a fine brown crust.

Serve with dumplings à la Waldviertel and raw cabbage salad. (See *Waldviertler Knödel*, page 102, and *Roher Krautsalat*, page 100).

Badner Kotelleten

New York has its Central Park, Paris its Bois de Boulogne, — and Vienna has the *Wienerwald*. It is 1250 square kilometres of greenery, villages and vineyards situated west and south of the capital. To the city's 1·7 million inhabitants it offers nature's solace for the price of a ride on the streetcar.

Many people from other lands know the Wienerwald from the Johann Strauss waltz *Tales from the Vienna Woods*. But in fact the forest is more associated with Beethoven and Schubert. At Baden, a spa already known to the Romans, and situated in the south of the woodlands, the great Beethoven spent all of fifteen summers, returning again and again in the hope that its sulphuric springs might help his hearing. Here he wrote his *Missa Solemnis* and much of the 9th symphony. During his work Beethoven sometimes disappeared into the woods for days, and once he was even mistaken as a tramp. Indeed, when he was challenged by the police, his efforts to establish his identity as the great composer were greeted with such incredulity that they locked him up as a madman. Only the intercession of a fellow musician saved him from a night in custody.

Badner Kotelleten *(Pork chops Baden style)*

INGREDIENTS:

4 pork chops about 150g each
Salt
Cooking fat
40g butter
Some mushrooms
3 eggs
2 to 3 tablespoons milk
Lard
Pepper
Chopped parsley

METHOD:

Beat the chops, salt and dip them lightly into flour on both sides. Heat cooking fat and fry the chops about 7 minutes on each side until golden brown and cooked. Place on platter and keep warm.

Add butter to the remaining gravy in the pan, stir in some stock and pour over the chops.

Heat lard, and fry the finely sliced mushrooms and chopped parsley. When the mushrooms are soft, add the beaten eggs mixed with milk, and seasoned with salt and pepper.

When cooked, garnish the chops with the scrambled eggs and mushrooms. Serve with *straw* potatoes. (See *Strohkartoffel,* side dishes page 102).

Badener Koteletten *(pork chops Baden style)*
left background.
Backerbsensuppe *(pea soup)*,
centre foreground.
Strohkartoffel *(straw potatoes)*
left background.

94

VEAL

Kalbsvögerl *(Fried veal)*

INGREDIENTS:
4 veal escalopes about 150–180g each cut rather thin
200g minced meat
Salt
Pepper
2 onions
Chopped parsley
60g butter
Stock
Sour cream as required

METHOD:
Beat the escalopes, extending as large and thin as possible. Rub with salt and pepper and put aside.

Fry half of the chopped onion and parsley in 30g butter and spread this mixture on one side of the veal escalopes. Season minced meat with salt and pepper and spread over the escalopes. Roll each escalope up firmly and tie with a string. Dip lightly into flour and fry briefly in hot butter on all sides. Remove the meat from the frying pan, stir the remaining onion and parsley into the pan, add stock and sour cream, then put the escalopes back and simmer until tender. Serve with boiled rice and salad.

Eingemachtes Kalbfleisch *(Stewed veal)*

INGREDIENTS:
600g diced veal
200g green peas
200g diced carrots
200g cauliflower (broken into pieces)
Salt
Pepper
Grated nutmeg
Cooking fat
Stock
40g butter
20g flour
Chopped parsley
Some mushrooms

METHOD:
Fry the diced meat briefly in hot cooking fat, add the vegetables and pour in some stock. Season with salt, pepper and nutmeg and simmer until tender.

Meanwhile heat butter and fry the finely sliced mushrooms and the chopped parsley. Finally stir in flour and a little bit of stock to get a smooth thick sauce. Add this to the meat, bring to the boil again and serve.

Serve with breadcrumb dumplings. (See *Bröselknödel*, side dishes page 99).

Paprikahenderl *(Chicken in paprika sauce)*

INGREDIENTS:
1 chicken
2 tablespoons oil
3 large onions
1 to 2 tablespoons paprika
1 tablespoon tomato purée
Some stock
3 to 4 tablespoons sour cream
1 level tablespoon flour

METHOD:
Cut the chicken into pieces, rub with salt and leave to stand for an hour. Heat cooking fat in a pan and fry the chopped onion without browning. Add the chicken, fry briefly on all sides in order to colour it, then sprinkle with paprika and pour in the stock. Add the tomato purée, stirring, then simmer until the chicken is soft. Mix sour cream with flour, add to the meat, bring to the boil again and serve. Serve with rice or sliced polenta. (See *Polentaschnitten*, side dishes page 100).

Paprikahenderl *(chicken in paprika sauce)* left.
Polentaschnitten *(polenta slices)*, right centre.
Gebackene Mäuse *(fried "mice")* background left.

96

MUTTON

Gedünstetes Schöps *(Stewed mutton)*

INGREDIENTS:
1kg shoulder of mutton
Cooking fat
120g carrots
120g parsley root
60g celery
10 peppercorns
1 bay leaf
1 level teaspoon ginger
1 onion
1 level tablespoon sugar
Stock
Salt and pepper to taste
3 tablespoons sour cream
1 to 2 tablespoons red wine
2 level tablespoons flour

METHOD:
Heat cooking fat and fry the finely cut root vegetables and chopped onion without browning. Add sugar and continue frying until it gets slightly yellow. Add all spices and the meat cut into neat pieces. Pour in the stock and simmer until the meat is soft.

Remove the mutton from the pan, place on a platter and keep warm. Mix sour cream, red wine and flour. Stir this mixture into the gravy, bring to the boil again, remove from the cooker, pass through a sieve and pour over the meat.

Serve with semolina dumplings. (See *Schwemmknödel*, side dishes page 100).

VENISON

Rehfilet in Apfelsauce

As has already been mentioned, venison was in earlier centuries a delicacy reserved for the nobility, who monopolised deer hunting, and indulged in many a feast when the hunting season was at its height.

However, even in mediaeval times, the nobility could not spend too much on pleasure because of heavy taxation on their estates. Particularly punitive to castle owners was the introduction of a building tax, which sometimes made it financially impossible for a family to enjoy a summer residence in the countryside. In these circumstances many simply removed the roofs from their castles, since without a roof a structure was no longer classified as a building. That is why today the Wachau hills are crowned by so many castle ruins. But it is still possible to wine and dine like a king.

Rehfilet in Apfelsauce
(Fillet of venison in apple sauce)

INGREDIENTS:
4 fillets of well-hung venison
Salt
Pepper
80g butter
Some stock

INGREDIENTS for the apple sauce:
3 slightly sour apples
1 tablespoon butter
2 level tablespoons flour
6 to 7 tablespoons beef broth or stock
Juice of 1 lemon
Sugar to taste

METHOD:
Beat the fillets lightly and season with salt and pepper. Heat butter and fry the fillets on both sides until brown and cooked. Arrange on a platter and keep warm. Add 2 to 3 tablespoons of stock to the butter gravy and pour over the meat.

Peel, core and slice the apples. Heat butter, add the apples and stew until soft. Stir in the flour and add beef broth or stock to get a thick sauce. Bring to the boil, add lemon juice and some sugar. Remove from heat and serve separately in a gravy boat. (See side dish *Kartoffelpuffer page 101*).

SIDE DISHES

Böhmische Knödel *(Bohemian dumplings)*

INGREDIENTS:
200g flour
1 egg
Water
Salt
4 stale rolls
30g butter

METHOD:
Mix flour, egg and salt, adding in as much water as necessary to get a medium firm dough. Put aside.

Heat butter, and fry the finely diced rolls or white bread until crisp and golden brown. Add to the dough and mix well. On a floured board shape the dough into cylinders 4 inches long and 2 inches diameter. Boil the dough-cylinders in salted water, drain and cut into slices about 1 inch thick.

Bröselknödel *(Breadcrumb dumplings)*

INGREDIENTS:
2 tablespoons butter
1 egg
1 stale roll moistened in milk and squeezed
Breadcrumbs as required
Salt
Pepper
Grated nutmeg
Chopped parsley

METHOD:
Cream butter and egg until fluffy. Add the roll, moistened in milk and squeezed. Season with salt, pepper and nutmeg, and stir in the parsley. Add sufficient breadcrumbs to get a medium to firm dough. Form small balls of about 1 inch diameter and cook gently in salted boiling water. Try cooking one dumpling first, and if the dough is not firm enough, add some more breadcrumbs.

Krautknödel *(Cabbage dumplings)*

INGREDIENTS:
1 small head of white cabbage
50g butter
2 eggs
1 tablespoon flour
Grated nutmeg
Salt

METHOD:
Cut the head of cabbage into squares, remove all stalks and cook in salted water until tender. Drain, squeeze out the liquid, and chop. Put aside and allow to cool.

Meanwhile cream butter and egg until fluffy, stir in the spices and flour, then add the cold chopped cabbage. If necessary, add some more flour to get a mixture which can be formed into balls of about 1½ inches diameter. Leave to stand for quarter of an hour, then simmer in plenty of boiling salted water until done.

Polentaschnitten *(Sliced polenta)*

INGREDIENTS:
250g maize grits
1¼l. (about 2 pints) water
Butter
Salt

METHOD:
Salt the water, bring to the boil and stir in the maize grits. Cook over a medium heat, stirring constantly. When thick, remove from heat and leave to cool for a bit. Prepare a board, and when still warm, place the maize mixture on to it.

With wet hands shape into a cylinder, and allow to get completely cold. Then with a wet knife or thread cut into slices of about ¾ inch thickness, and fry in hot butter.

Roher Krautsalat *(Raw cabbage salad)*

INGREDIENTS:
500g shredded white cabbage
⅛l. (approx. 4 fl.ozs) watered wine vinegar
Salt
Pepper
Caraway
Sugar to taste
1 finely chopped onion
3 tablespoons oil

METHOD:
Pour the vinegar into a pot, add the spices and bring to the boil. Simmer for some minutes. Mix the cabbage with the finely chopped onion and pour the hot vinegar over the salad. Cover and leave to stand until cold. Before serving, add oil and sugar to taste, and mix well.

(Excellent with roasted or fried pork and any kind of dumpling.)

Schwemmknödel *(Semolina dumplings)*

INGREDIENTS:
3 eggs
2 tablespoons butter
1 tablespoon sour cream
250g semolina
Salt
Pepper
Chopped parsley

METHOD:
Cream butter and eggs until fluffy. Add salt, pepper and parsley. Then stir in the semolina. Add some sour cream to get a soft-to-medium dough. Leave to stand for an hour, when the dough should be medium-to-firm. Form balls and cook in plenty of salted water until they rise to the surface (approx. 15 minutes). Simmer for a few more minutes, then cut one dumpling into halves to test for readiness.

POTATO SIDE DISHES

Austrian cuisine is rich in potato dishes. Perhaps that is because the country still remembers what it owes to this particular plant . . .

The potato probably came to Austria around 1590. Certainly in 1683 Wolf Helmhard von Hoberg was already mentioning potato salad in his recipe collection. But it was relatively unknown amongst the wider public, despite the fact that Empress Maria Theresa herself tried to make it popular.

Things changed after 1761, during the Seven Years War between Prussia and Austria. The dynamic priest Johann Eberhard Jungblut had brought seed potatoes from the Netherlands to the *Weinviertel,* and when he planted them local farmers made jokes about the "strange" growths in the cleric's garden. But when the region was afflicted by famine in the years that followed, only the potato prevented starvation. Soon it was being planted throughout the Weinviertel, and by and by became familiar to the other Austrian regions as well.

Hauerknödel *(Vintager's dumplings)*

INGREDIENTS:
Raw potatoes
Flour as required
Salt

METHOD:
Grate the raw peeled potatoes into a bowl and mix with sufficient flour to get a medium firm dough. With wet hands quickly form balls of about 2 inches diameter, dip into flour and cook in plenty of boiling water, lifting the dumplings with a spoon now and then, so that they do not stick to the bottom of the pot.

After 10 to 15 minutes cut one dumpling in half to test if cooked. Drain and serve.

Kartoffelpuffer *(Scooped potatoes)*

INGREDIENTS:
1kg potatoes
3 eggs
2 tablespoons sour cream
50g flour
Pinch of salt
Cooking fat

METHOD:
Peel and grate the raw potatoes, put them into a kitchen cloth and press out all the liquid. Mix with beaten eggs, flour, sour cream and salt.

Heat cooking fat in a large frying pan until very hot. With a tablespoon scoop out portions of the potato mixture and, depending on the size of the pan, place 3 or 4 portions in the hot fat. With the spoon press them flat, shaping each into an irregular disc. Fry on both sides until golden brown.

Strohkartoffel *(Straw potatoes)*

INGREDIENTS:
Potatoes
Cooking fat or oil
Salt

METHOD:
Peel the raw potatoes and cut them as finely as vermicelli. Dry with absorbent paper and fry in deep cooking fat until golden brown. Drain, salt and serve immediately.

Waldviertler Knödel *(Dumplings Waldviertel style)*

INGREDIENTS:
1kg potatoes
Salt

METHOD:
Peel and boil half of the potatoes. When still hot, grate them and spread on a board to dry overnight. On the next day grate the remaining raw potatoes, put them into a kitchen cloth and press out all the liquid into a bowl. Mix the boiled and unboiled potatoes. Allow the liquid in the bowl to get clear and to form a starch sediment at the bottom. Then pour off the clear liquid very cautiously and add the starch at the bottom to the potato mixture. Mix well and form balls of about 1½ inches diameter. Put them into boiling water and simmer for about 20–25 minutes very gently. (If the water is boiling too much, the dumplings will fall apart). While simmering turn over the dumplings once to twice to make sure that they do not stick to the bottom.

Strohkartoffel *(straw potatoes)*

DESSERTS

Waldviertler Mohnnudeln

This dish, also called *Black Michael*, is a typical speciality of the Waldviertel. In former times it was mainly prepared for the Christmas Eve dinner.

Despite the poor soil of the region, — a huge plateau about 2,500 feet above sea level, — most of the people still make their living from farming, and to make life a little bit easier, a distribution of farm products was organised. Under this every farmer sells a certain speciality, such as home-made marinated pork, bacon, ham or bread, directly to the consumer. The idea has now become well-established, as have the old recipes, which guests and tourists are discovering to their great delight.

Waldviertler Mohnnudeln
(Potato noodles with poppy seed)

INGREDIENTS:
500g potatoes
50g butter
1 egg
Pinch of salt
150g flour
200g ground poppy seed
50g sugar
30g butter
Some milk mixed with rum
Sifted sugar

METHOD:
Boil the potatoes in their jackets, drain, peel and mash while still hot.

Mix the mashed potatoes with butter, egg, flour and a pinch of salt and prepare a rather firm dough. Form the dough into strands on a board, cut off small portions about 1½ inches long and of ½ inch diameter, pointed at their ends. Simmer in salted water until the potato noodles float to the surface, drain, and while still in the sieve, rinse briefly in cold water.

Melt butter in a frying pan, add the ground poppy seed, sugar, and 1 to 2 tablespoons milk mixed with rum. Place the noodles into the mixture, and stir gently until they are covered with poppy seed. Put into a bowl, sprinkle generously with sifted sugar and serve.

Ödenburger Nudeln

The town of Ödenburg, particularly known for the red wine produced in its own neighbourhood, appears in the history books under its Germanic name as early as 856. It is situated south-east of Vienna, and up to 1918 the majority of its inhabitants were German-speaking. But after the demise of the Austrian Empire, it became a Hungarian town called Sopron.

Ödenburger Nudeln *(Noodles Odenburg style)*

INGREDIENTS:
150g noodles
½l. (approx. 18 fl. ozs) milk
120g ground poppy seed
40g butter
2 to 3 tablespoons raisins
Sugar and cinnamon to taste
50g butter
3 eggs
80g sugar mixed with vanilla sugar

METHOD:
Cook the noodles in boiling water until soft, and drain. Meanwhile cook the ground poppy seed together with butter, raisins, sugar and cinnamon in milk, and leave to cool.

Cream 50g butter and 80g sugar until fluffy and gradually add the egg yolks. Finally fold in the stiffly whisked egg whites and mix this with the noodles.

Grease an ovenware dish and place alternate layers of noodles and poppy seed mixture into it, beginning and ending with noodles. Bake in a medium oven for half an hour and serve.

Pfirsichknödel in Topfenteig *(Peach dumplings)*

INGREDIENTS:
250g curds
5 tablespoons flour
40g margarine
1 egg
Pinch of salt
80g butter
100g breadcrumbs
Sifted sugar
Peaches or plums

METHOD:
Mix flour, curds, margarine, egg and a pinch of salt into a dough, and leave to stand for at least half-an-hour. Work the dough into strands, cut off equal portions and with wet hands press each portion flat into discs the size of your palm.

Put a plum or peach in the centre of each disc. Wrap the fruit in the dough and form into balls. Cook gently in boiling water for about 15 minutes. Drain and roll through breadcrumbs fried in butter. Put on a platter and sprinkle with sifted sugar.

Wachauer Marillenknödel

There is no doubt that the female population of the Wachau knows how to handle the kitchen spoon, — and as the following anecdote shows, it is an aptitude which occasionally finds expression outwith the scope of their delicious regional dishes.

In the township of Krems there is a monument called the *Simandl-Brunnen*, or Simandl fountain. It shows a man dressed in a mediaeval gown, kneeling in front of his wife, asking for the key to his home.

According to legend, the man depicted was Simon Handl, who was frequently beaten with the cooking spoon for spending the nights in a wine tavern. So as not to be locked out, he asks for the key on his knees. Since then *Simandl* has become the expression throughout Austria for a hen-pecked man, replacing the German word *Pantoffelheld*, also meaning *hen-pecked*, and still used in Germany and Switzerland.

Wachauer Marillenknödel
(Apricot dumplings à la Wachau)

INGREDIENTS:
500g potatoes
100–150g flour
1 tablespoon semolina
1 egg
Pinch of salt
250 to 300g apricots
100g breadcrumbs
80g butter
Sifted sugar

METHOD:

Boil the potatoes in their jackets, drain and peel. While still hot, either sieve or mash, and mix with semolina. Leave to cool. When almost cold, spread on a baking board, mix with flour, egg, a pinch of salt, and knead into a rather firm dough.

Work the dough into strands, cut off equal portions and press each portion with wet hands into discs the size of one's palm.

Make an incision in each apricot, remove the stone and replace with a piece of lump sugar. Press the apricots together again and place one fruit in the middle of each disc of dough. Wrap the apricots with the dough by shaping into balls. Boil in salted water for about 10 minutes.

The dumpling should then be fried in butter. When cooked, drain and gently roll 2 or 3 at a time in the fried breadcrumbs. Put on to a platter and sprinkle generously with sifted sugar.

Wachauer Marillenknödel *(apricot dumplings à la Wachau)*.

Wachauer Torte (Gateau Wachau style)

INGREDIENTS:
140g sugar
7 egg yolks
7 egg whites
140g ground almonds
70g chocolate
1 to 2 tablespoons breadcrumbs

INGREDIENTS for the filling:
1 egg
120g butter
100g chocolate
Sugar to taste

METHOD:

Cream egg yolks and sugar until fluffy, and add alternately melted or grated chocolate and ground almonds. Gently stir in the stiffly whisked egg whites and breadcrumbs with a kitchen spoon. Fill the mixture into a well-greased and floured cake tin, and bake in a medium oven. Leave to cool overnight.

Cut the gateau horizontally into two, spread the bottom half with the filling and put together again. Spread the remaining filling on the top and sides.

METHOD for the filling:

Cream butter and beaten egg until fluffy, add the melted chocolate and sugar to taste. Put into refrigerator, stirring now and then whilst it cools.

Griess-Auflauf (Semolina pudding)

INGREDIENTS:
150g semolina
½l. (approx. 18fl.ozs) milk
70g butter
3 eggs
150g sugar
Raisins

METHOD:

Bring the milk to the boil and stir in the semolina. Keep stirring constantly until it thickens, then remove from heat and leave to cool.

Meanwhile cream butter and sugar until fluffy and gradually stir in the egg yolks and a handful of raisins. Fold in alternately the stiffly whisked egg whites and the cold semolina mixture. Put this in a well-greased baking tin and bake in a medium oven.

Serve with compote.

Weinkoch (Wine pudding)

INGREDIENTS:
5 eggs
120g sugar
100g breadcrumbs
Cinnamon
1½l. (approx. 2½ pints) wine
Piece of cinnamon rind
Some cloves
Some sugar to taste

METHOD:

Cream egg yolks and sugar until fluffy. Season with salted cinnamon, and gently fold in the stiffly whisked egg whites and breadcrumbs. Bake in a well-greased mould in a medium oven and invert into a bowl. Boil the wine with cinnamon rind, cloves and sugar to taste for about 10 minutes. Pour over the pudding and put the bowl into refrigerator. Serve very cold.

Weincremenocken (Dumplings in wine sauce)

INGREDIENTS:
a) 4 egg whites
140g sifted sugar

b) ¾l. (approx. 1¼ pints) white wine
Vanilla sugar
Piece of cinnamon rind
3 cloves
1 lemon slice
40g sugar

c) 4 egg yolks
60g sugar

METHOD:

a) Whisk the egg whites until very stiff. Gently stir in the sifted sugar and put in refrigerator.

b) Heat white wine in a large casserole. Add sugar and vanilla sugar, cinnamon rind, cloves and lemon slice. Cook for 10 minutes, then reduce heat. With a tablespoon scoop out portions of the whisked egg whites, and place them at intervals into the hot wine. Simmer very gently for about two minutes, turn over and cook the other side. Then remove the dumplings from the wine and place 2 or 3 per person on small plates and leave to cool.

c) Cream egg yolks and sugar until fluffy. Stirring constantly, add the hot wine slowly and continue beating until the sauce is cold. Cover the dumplings with the sauce, and serve.

Desserts Fried in Lard

Desserts fried in lard are typical of the Austrian countryside, and can be served either warm or cold. They are among the oldest traditional dishes, dating back at least 1,000 years, to the days when they would be prepared in a cast iron pot on an open fire, as indeed they would be prepared when Richard Coeur de Lion was a prisoner at Dürnstein.

Shall we dine with the Lionheart? Why not, if you serve the following two dishes?

Gebackene Mäuse *(Fried "mice")*

INGREDIENTS:
300g flour
30g yeast
⅛l. (approx. 4fl.ozs) lukewarm milk
2 eggs
50g sugar
50g butter
1 tablespoon rum
Some raisins
Cooking fat for frying
Sifted sugar

METHOD:
Place flour mixed with a pinch of salt in a basin, and make a hole in the middle. Dissolve the yeast in some lukewarm milk and pour into the hole. Cover with some flour and allow to rise.

Meanwhile cream butter, eggs and sugar until fluffy, and add rum and raisins. Stir this into the yeast mixture, add milk and work with a wooden spoon into a dough. Beat the dough until it comes off the sides of the basin. Leave to stand for half-an-hour to rise again.

Scoop out portions with a tablespoon and fry in deep hot cooking fat on both sides until golden brown. Drain and sprinkle generously with sifted sugar. Serve with coffee.

Schmalzstrauben *(Yeast cake fried in lard)*

INGREDIENTS:
600g flour
120g butter
20g yeast
100g sugar
1 egg
Pinch of salt
¾l. (approx. 26 fl.ozs) milk
Hot lard for frying
Sugar mixed with cinnamon
Hot raspberry syrup

METHOD:
Mix milk and flour into a smooth paste, add sugar and stir in the crumbled yeast. Add the softened butter and the beaten eggs. Then put in a warm place and leave to rise.

Heat plenty of lard, or cooking fat, in a pan, and pour the batter through a funnel into the lard, starting in the centre of the pan and spiralling outwards until it is full. Fry on both sides until golden brown and place on a wire rack to drain. Sprinkle with sugar mixed with some cinnamon, and serve with hot raspberry syrup.

CHAPTER FIVE

VISITING AUSTRIA'S
TRADITIONAL HOLIDAY AREAS

The village of St. Wolfgang with the terrace of the White Horse Inn as foreground.

Salzburg has three associations which readily come to mind, — Mozart, *The Sound of Music* and *Salzburger Nockerl*. In the same way music and food characterise the lake region to the east of Austria's well-known festival town. The *Salzkammergut* was a traditional holiday region long before the Salzburg season attracted visitors from all over the world.

Specifically the Salzkammergut forms part of three Austrian provinces, — Salzburg, Styria and Upper Austria, the latter comprising the largest area. Although each has its own character and its own specialities, they form a unit with the township of Bad Ischl as the centre.

Surrounded by about 20 lakes, both large and small, the spa Bad Ischl is more than just a place for leisure. The composers Anton Bruckner, Johannes Brahms and Giacomo Meyerbeer, as frequent guests, set the region to music. Johann Strauss and Franz Lehar were its most prominent residents for many years. Emperor Francis Joseph I spent 83 summers of his life there, and it became the courting ground for his wooing of teenage Bavarian Princess Elisabeth, — later to be known as the popular Austrian Empress Sissi. A section of the Emperor's summer residence is still inhabited by one of his descendants.

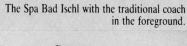

The Spa Bad Ischl with the traditional coach in the foreground.

But paying respects to the country's imperial period, — or even attending the annual Lehar operetta performances, — are not the only attractions for the tourist in Bad Ischl. More than anything else, the highlight of the visit could be to have a gateau or a strudel, an ice-cream or a cup of coffee at *Zauner's*. This confectioner's shop is almost as famous as the Spanish Riding School or the Vienna Opera House. From the finest cake right down to the smallest praline, everything offered at Zauner's is still hand-made.

Then on the shore of the nearby Wolfgangsee is the White Horse Inn, world-renowned for its Benatzky operetta of the same name. From there a rack-railway leads to the *Schafberg,* offering a magnificent view over the region.

Entrance to the White Horse Inn
(Weisses Rössl).

In the south, the *Hallstättersee* provides evidence of European history going back at least 4,000 years. In the picturesque and romantic village of Hallstatt, attached to the rocks like a bird's nest, objects of the earliest Iron Age culture were first identified. In the Hallstatt salt mine, considered to be the oldest in Europe, was found the body of a prehistoric miner, fully clothed with all his implements. He had been completely preserved in the salt.

At another salt mine, in Altaussee, in the Styrian part of the Salzkammergut, Adolf Hitler hid the valuables he had collected from various parts of Europe. The atmospheric conditions were found to be ideal for paintings and statues, whilst the mine also proved a secure hiding place for other treasures, such as gold reserves and prototype weapons developed by the Third Reich.

The market square of Hallstatt — a place with a 4,000 year old history.

However, the beautiful Altaussee and Bad Aussee villages, with their neat and pretty houses, are famous for quite a different reason. One of Austria's most romantic love stories had its setting in this region. Prince John of Hapsburg, the younger brother of Emperor Francis I, fell in love with Anna Plochl, the daughter of a Bad Aussee postmaster. After 10 years of procrastination his imperial brother finally gave Prince John permission to marry her. Later Anna was made Countess of Meran.

This happened away back in 1829, but Anna Plochl's cookery book is still in existence, and was on public display at the bi-centenary of Prince John's birth.

Apart from the Salzkammergut, the Carinthian lake region is considered traditional Austrian holiday country. Bounded on the north by Grossglockner, Austria's highest mountain, and on the south by the rugged Karnic Alps and Karawanken along the Italian and Yugoslavian borders, it provides marvellous opportunities for water sports as well as for hiking and mountain climbing. The Grossglockner has also our largest glacier.

So many of the castles are not only relics of ancient history, but have found a role and a function in this present day, being either converted into restaurants like the Castle of Landskron, or like the Porcia Renaissance castle in the town of Spittal, used for open air theatre performances. Monasteries like Millstatt and Ossiach, both situated on lakes of the same respective names, are exquisite backgrounds for concerts and choirs before which world famous conductors like Leonard Bernstein have performed.

The town of Villach is surrounded by lakes, and is recognised as Austria's gateway to the south. Bright Renaissance buildings, with their arcades and balconies, dominate its main squares. The nearby thermal springs of Warmbad Villach were used by the Romans, and in his day Napoleon wanted to convert it into the biggest spa in Europe. He failed for lack of time, but eventually it did develop into a holiday resort offering everything from sport to leisure trails. Expansive parklands surround the elegant hotels, and the rich farmlands which supply the meat, fruit and vegetables are never more than a few hundred yards from the kitchens.

Individual valleys vary widely in traditions and regional costumes, and one is rarely more than an hour's hike from an inexpensive family run *Gasthof* where the daughter of the house serves Carinthian *Fleischnudeln* or *Frigga*, or perhaps the *yellow* soup special to her region.

So art and music, delicious food and Mother Nature in her most benign mood, all combine to bring about an atmosphere of enjoyable tranquillity, — an atmosphere which can nevertheless be created in your own home with the help of some Carinthian choir music from the *Madrigal-choir* or *Singkreis Porcia*, whose records are sold throughout Europe, and which will provide a suitable background for the recommended dishes.

A typical pub in the village of Altaussee, where Austria's most romantic love story happened.

113

SOUPS

Wasserhennensuppe

   This soup, which has a long tradition in the Salzkammergut, has no connection with chickens. Nobody really knows where the name originates, and it is probably one of the numerous "beloved oddities" peculiar to one particular Austrian province.

Wasserhennensuppe *("Water-chicken" soup)*

INGREDIENTS:
4 to 6 stale rolls
60–80g butter or lard
2 eggs
Milk
Pinch of salt
Margarine or lard for greasing a casserole
Beef broth or stock

METHOD:
   Slice the rolls very thin, pour over hot butter or lard, then add the beaten eggs combined with some milk. Salt, and leave to stand for about 15 minutes.
   Place the mixture in a well-greased casserole and put into a medium oven. When the surface starts to get golden brown, tear apart with a fork into irregular pieces. Pour over some melted butter, and continue baking until golden brown. Then empty into a soup tureen and add the stock or beef broth.

Faschpofesensuppe (Upper Austria)
(Soup with minced meat toast)

INGREDIENTS:
2 egg yolks
250g minced meat
1 stale roll moistened in milk and squeezed
50g butter
Salt
Pepper
Nutmeg
3 stale rolls
Milk
2 eggs
Cooking fat

Cream butter and egg yolks until fluffy. Add the moistened roll along with salt, pepper, grated nutmeg and finally the minced meat. Work into a smooth mixture.

Cut the 3 other rolls into thin slices, (about ¼ inch thick), spread half the slices with the meat mixture, and cover with the remaining slices to form a sandwich.

Dip each sandwich into milk, then into the beaten eggs, and fry in hot deep cooking fat on both sides.

Put in a soup tureen, and pour over with hot beef broth or stock.

Gmundner Kirchtagsuppe

Gmunden, at the northern shore of the Traunsee, was in the 13th century a wealthy township because of its salt trading. Towards the end of the 18th century, when the salt trade was no longer important, it became more and more famous as a holiday resort for the nobility, the upper class and artists. The German Emperor Frederick III and the King of Württemberg spent the summer season there, and it was also frequented by the composers Schubert and Brahms.

Particularly renowned for its beauty is the lake-castle *Schloss Ort,* dating from the 11th century, where the Hapsburg prince, John Salvator, lived until his disappearance in 1880 on a sailing expedition off the coast of South America. Today Gmunden and the various other villages around the Traunsee, — once known to the Romans as the *lacus felix* or *happy lake,* — are amongst the main holiday resorts in the Salzkammergut.

Gmundner Kirchtagsuppe
(Feast-day soup Gmunden style)

INGREDIENTS:
500g game
100g root vegetables
Salt
Peppercorns
Cloves
1 bay leaf
Juniper berries
50g bacon
20g margarine
60g flour
⅛l. (approx. 4 fl. ozs) sour cream
1 chopped onion
⅛l. (approx. 4 fl. ozs) red wine

METHOD:
Put the game together with the spices into a pot, adding about 4 pints of salted water, bring to the boil and simmer for some 2 hours. Drain and dice the meat before setting aside to cool. Heat margarine, and fry the chopped onion and the finely chopped root vegetables together with the diced bacon until golden brown. Stir in the flour, and gradually add the soup and the red wine. Simmer for about 15 minutes, then pass through a sieve. Heat up again, add sour cream and diced meat and serve.

Sunset in the lake region of the Salzkammergut.

115

Mondseer Fischsuppe

The region around the Mondsee, — one of the large Salzkammergut lakes, — was already inhabited during the lake-dwelling era. The township of Mondsee came into being after Bavaria founded a Benedictine monastery there in 748. A speciality of the region is *Mondsee-cheese*.

Mondseer Fischsuppe
(Fish soup Mondsee style)

INGREDIENTS:
500g river or lake fish
1l. (1¾ pints) water
Salt
Lemon juice
1 or 2 parsley roots
½ head of celery
⅛l. (approx. 4 fl. ozs) white wine
Chopped dill
1 bay leaf
1 onion

METHOD:

Gut and clean the fish in cold water, flavour with lemon juice and leave to stand for 5 minutes.

Heat salted water, add the sliced onion and bay leaf and bring to the boil. Add the fish, reduce heat and simmer for about 10 minutes until the fish is cooked. Remove the fish and put aside.

Peel the parsley roots and grate them together with the celery. Add to the soup and simmer without boiling for 5 minutes. Add white wine and the fish, broken into pieces. Heat up, add chopped dill and serve.

Rahmsuppe *(Sour cream soup)*

INGREDIENTS:
¼l. (approx. 9fl. ozs) sour cream
30g flour
Caraway
Salt
Chopped chive
1l. (approx. 1¾ pints) stock

METHOD:

Heat stock with caraway and salt. Bring to the boil and simmer for some minutes. Mix flour and sour cream and stir into the soup. Continue to simmer for 1 or 2 minutes, then remove from heat and add the chopped chive. Serve with diced white bread fried in butter.

Gelbe Gailtaler Kirchtagsuppe

A village feast day or *kermis* is always a great social event. Nowhere is it more picturesque than in the Gail Valley of Southern Carinthia, inhabited by both Austrians and Slovenes since mediaeval times, so that two different cultures meet there, each with its own national costume. At the same time venerated traditions, kept alive, sustain customs, songs and dishes which are quite different from those found in other regions.

The *feast-day* or *yellow soup* is one such speciality, — served only in parts of Carinthia, — but also available at home if made to the following recipe:

Gelbe Gailtaler Kirchtagsuppe
(Yellow soup of the Gail Valley)

INGREDIENTS:
1kg meat
  (various pieces of chicken, mutton, beef)
Some bones
1 small piece of liver
Salt
2 leeks
1 clove of garlic
1 bay leaf
Thyme
Rosemary
30g flour
⅜l. (approx. 13 fl. ozs) sour cream
1 teaspoon vinegar
1 or 2 egg yolks
Pinch of saffron
Diced white bread fried in butter

METHOD:
Put the meat, bones, liver, salt, garlic, bay leaf, rosemary and thyme into 1½l. (2½ pints) of cold water, bring to the boil and gently simmer until the meat is soft.

Drain and put the clear soup back into the pot. Dice the meat and drop it in. Stir in vinegar, saffron and the sour cream mixed with flour. Bring to the boil, then remove from heat. Add the egg yolks, stir well and serve with the diced bread fried in butter.

A typical Carinthian farmhouse.

Leberpüreesuppe *(Liverpurée soup)*

INGREDIENTS:
100g chopped bacon
250g liver
150g to 200g root vegetables
1 small onion
1 tablespoon flour
1½l. (2½ pints) stock or beef broth
Salt
Pepper
Mustard
Some sugar
Teaspoon vinegar
3 tablespoons sour cream
Parsley
Diced white bread fried in butter

METHOD:
Chop the onion and cut the root vegetables into fine strips, the liver into thin slices.

Fry the chopped bacon without browning, then add onion, root vegetables and liver. Continue frying until the liver is cooked. Stir in the flour and fry for some minutes. Remove from heat and put into the blender in order to work all ingredients into a purée.

Put the purée into a pot, add stock or beef broth and bring to the boil. Add vinegar, mustard, sugar, salt, pepper and chopped parsley. Finally stir in sour cream, remove from heat and serve with diced soft bread previously fried in butter.

Main street of Bad Ischl, where the second last Austrian Emperor spent 83 summers of his life.

118

STARTERS

Culinary weeks and the Club of Carinthian Cooks

Of the many lakes in Carinthia the *Millstättersee* and the *Wörthersee* are the most famous. They have been recognised as classical holiday playgrounds for more than a hundred years. Perhaps the ten-mile-long Wörthersee is better known internationally with its main holiday resorts of Pörtschach and Velden and the lovely Maria Wörth peninsula, which have earned it the title of the *Austrian Riviera*. It is spectacular and elegant, offering all kinds of water sports, horse riding, international shows and a casino, as well as the most exclusive hotels and nightbars.

The *Millstättersee,* however, is much more romantic. Apart from its sports, it is a paradise for hikers and individualists who prefer smaller hotels, old traditions, concerts and choir music, such as one hears performed at the township of Millstatt. Farmhouse holidays are a popular feature of this region, and contact with the local population is easily established. As a gesture to gourmets, Millstatt instituted *culinary weeks,* during which every restaurant serves its different specialities.

At the same time *The Club of Carinthian Cooks,* founded in 1973, aims to promote Carinthian cuisine by training apprentices, and creating new and delicate variations of local dishes. Its success is obvious. Thus far at international cooking competitions *the club* has won 57 gold, 15 silver, and 5 bronze medals. The following 4 recipes are typical of their respective regions.

Open-air casino at the Wörthersee in Carinthia.

Lebertoast Millstatt (Liver toast Millstatt style)

INGREDIENTS:
½kg liver
200g onions
100g butter
⅛l. (approx. 4 fl. ozs) sour cream
1 teaspoon cranberries
1 teaspoon tomato purée
Paprika
Curry powder
Pepper
Salt
1 tablespoon brandy or cognac

METHOD:
Cut the liver into inch by half-inch slices. Put into a sieve and run under cold water. Leave to drain. Heat butter, and fry the finely chopped onions until golden brown. Add the liver and fry until cooked, stirring very gently. Stir in sour cream, tomato purée and cranberries. Season with salt and spices and stir in or flambé with brandy.

Put on hot toast and serve immediately.

Millstätter Seejungfräulein (Mermaid Millstatt style)

INGREDIENTS:
4 lake or river fish according to season
⅛l. (approx. 4 fl. ozs) white wine
⅛l. (approx. 4 fl. ozs) cream
Flour
Salt
Pepper
Paprika
Curry
1 medium-sized onion
Chopped dill
Parsley
Juice of 1 lemon
2 to 3 tablespoons dry sherry
2 egg yolks

METHOD:
Gut and clean the fish. Place them in a casserole and sprinkle with salt, pepper, chopped onion and chopped dill, paprika and chopped parsley. Add the white wine and lemon juice and stew gently for 10 minutes. Leave to cool.

Remove the fish from the casserole and skin them. Put aside. Mix cream with some flour and stir into the fish sauce. Bring to the boil, reduce heat and add egg yolks and sherry. Put the fish back, heat up without boiling, sprinkle with curry, then arrange on a platter and serve.

Bries in Sherrysauce (Sweetbreads in sherry sauce)

INGREDIENTS:
750g sweetbreads
Salt
Pepper
Sage
Butter
0·4 l. (approx. 14 fl. ozs) dry sherry
1 gravy cube dissolved in ⅛l. (approx. 4 fl. ozs) water
¼l. (approx. 9 fl. ozs) cream
1 tablespoon tarragon leaves

METHOD:
Immerse the sweetbreads for a few seconds in boiling water to which vinegar has been added. Then drain and skin.

Pluck into neat pieces, sprinkle with salt, pepper and grated sage. Dip into flour and quickly fry in hot butter. Add the sherry, the cream and the gravy cube dissolved in water. Simmer until the sweetbread is cooked and the sauce slightly reduced and medium thick. Finally add a tablespoon of tarragon leaves and serve with boiled rice.

Gefüllte Wörtherseeforelle (Stuffed trout Wörthersee style)

INGREDIENTS:
1 trout per person
Some minced veal
Salt
Pepper
Crushed garlic
White wine
⅜l. (approx. 7 fl. ozs) sour cream
30g butter
Caraway
4 tablespoons white wine
40g crayfish tail

METHOD:
Gut and bone the trout. Stuff with minced veal seasoned with salt, pepper and ½ crushed clove of garlic. Put the stuffed trout in a pan, add the white wine and stew until cooked. Drain and set aside.

Heat butter in a pan. Mix 4 tablespoons of white wine with cream, season with salt and caraway and add to the butter. Bring to the boil, add the crayfish tail, cover and simmer for 20 minutes. If the sauce gets too much reduced, add some of the white wine in which the trout has been stewed. Finally heat up the trout in the sauce, and serve.

Liesertaler Hechtschnitte

The valley of the Lieser extends from the Millstättersee northwards towards the Alps. This is the hikers' paradise, with endless meadows, and slopes with soft green terraces halfway between the valley and the mountain summits.

The main township Gmünd still looks as it was in mediaeval times, with its cobbled streets and quaint old buildings, crowned by a huge castle ruin.

Liesertaler Hechtschnitte
(Pike fillet Liesertal style)

INGREDIENTS:
4 fillets of pike, each 150 to 180g
Brown breadcrumbs
Bacon cut into strips for larding
½l. (approx. 18 fl.ozs) sour cream,
4 dried pears
12 medium sized potatoes
Fish spices
Chopped parsley
Cooking fat

METHOD:
Flake, season and lard the fillets. Then roll them in brown breadcrumbs and fry in hot deep cooking fat until crisp.

Boil the potatoes in their jackets, drain and peel. Mix sour cream with the finely chopped parsley and the finely diced dried pears. Pour this sauce over the potatoes and serve together with the fish.

Sardellenkarpfen *(Carp with anchovies)*

INGREDIENTS:
4 fillets of carp of about 150 to 180g each
8 tinned anchovies
Flour
Butter
¼l. (approx. 9 fl. ozs) sour cream

METHOD:
Salt the fillets, dip into flour and fry in butter on both sides until done. Arrange on a platter and keep warm.

Chop the anchovies and stir into the remaining butter in the pan. (If too reduced add some more butter). Fry for 1 to 2 minutes, then add sour cream mixed with a teaspoon of flour. Bring to the boil, season with salt and pepper to taste, and pour the sauce over the carp fillets.

Bruckner Eier

This Upper Austrian speciality, also called *Eierfisch*, was the favourite starter of the composer Anton Bruckner, who came from the Upper Austrian village of Ansfelden.

Bruckner Eier
(Poached eggs Bruckner style)

INGREDIENTS:
A mixture of ⅔ vinegar and ⅓ water
Some peppercorns
Half a lemon
1 bay leaf
2 eggs per person
Salt
Pepper
Onions

METHOD:
Put the vinegar-water mixture into a pot, add the peppercorns, bay leaf and half lemon still in its skin. Bring to the boil. Carefully fold in the whole eggs and simmer until the egg whites are firm, while the yolks should stay soft.

Drain and arrange on a platter. Season with salt and pepper, pour over 1 to 2 tablespoons of the water-vinegar mixture and garnish with lots of sliced onions which have been fried in butter until golden brown.

Cheese producer in a mountain shed in the Alps.

Trout

Trout (*a traditional dish of the Salzkammergut*)

Trout was a favourite with both Goethe and Beethoven. The Austrian composer Franz Schubert even set it to music with his *Forellen-Quintett*.

In the Salzkammergut, with its many lakes, fish dishes are a staple part of the local cuisine. The Church of Traunkirchen on the Traunsee, for instance, has its pulpit shaped like a boat, and the wood carvings show St. Peter with his laden nets after the miracle on the Sea of Galilee.

Until the end of the 19th century a voyage on the Traunsee was the only means of travel from north to south, and the mountain range is so close to the lake that when a road was ultimately commissioned by Emperor Francis Joseph I, it had to be blasted through the rocks.

Forelle im Silberkleid (*Trout in silver dress*)

INGREDIENTS:
4 trout
Pepper
Salt
100g butter
4 tablespoons white wine
Dill
100g chopped almonds fried in butter

METHOD:
Gut and clean the trout, salt and pepper inside, and stuff with a bunch of dill. Place each trout on a sheet of foil. Mix the white wine with the melted butter and pour over the fish. Wrap up each trout and put into a rather hot oven. Bake for 15 minutes. Remove from foil, arrange the trout on an ovenware dish and sprinkle with chopped almonds fried in butter. Put the trout back into the oven and bake without foil until golden brown.

Gebackene Forellen (*Fried trout*)
INGREDIENTS:
4 trout
Salt
2 eggs
Flour
Breadcrumbs
Cooking fat
Parsley
1 sliced lemon

METHOD:
Gut and clean the trout. Salt inside and outside. Roll each trout in flour, dip into beaten eggs and coat with breadcrumbs. Fry in hot deep cooking fat on each side until golden brown. Garnish with parsley and lemon slices, serve with green salad and boiled potatoes tossed in butter and chopped parsley.

SMALL DISHES

Schinkenerdäpfel (Carinthia)
(Doughnuts with ham)

INGREDIENTS:
400g boiled potatoes
400g flour
30g yeast
4 eggs
Grated nutmeg
Cream as required
Finely chopped ham
Cooking fat

METHOD:
Boil the potatoes in their jackets, peel and mash. Put the flour into a bowl, make a hole in the centre and place therein the yeast dissolved in a little cream. Cover with flour and leave to stand for half-an-hour. Stir in the beaten eggs, nutmeg, pinch of salt and mix with the mashed potatoes into a dough.

Roll out the dough and cut out discs the size of your palm. Put finely chopped ham on half the discs and top with the other half. Pinch the rim firmly together and leave in a warm place to rise.

Fry the doughnuts in hot deep cooking fat and serve warm with a green salad.

Kärntner Krengericht
(Carinthian horse-radish dish)

INGREDIENTS:
1kg potatoes
40g butter
30g flour
½l. (approx. 18 fl.ozs) stock
⅛l. (approx. 4 fl. ozs) cream
½ grated horse-radish root
Some sugar
300g minced meat
1 egg
Salt
Pepper
1 clove of garlic
Marjoram
Breadcrumbs

METHOD:
Boil the potatoes in their jackets, drain and peel. Leave till cold and then slice. Put aside.

Heat butter, stir in flour and gradually add stock, then cream. Boil gently for about 10 minutes. Season with salt and sugar and stir in the grated horse-radish. Put aside.

Mix the minced meat with the beaten egg, season with salt, pepper, marjoram and the crushed garlic. Stir in some breadcrumbs and shape into little balls of about 1 inch diameter.

Put the sliced potatoes, together with the minced meat balls, into the horse-radish sauce and simmer for about 10 minutes, then serve.

Carinthian specialities Southern style

Carinthian noodles, either filled with curd-mixture or with minced meat, is a traditional dish cooked only in Carinthia and, with variations, in the adjoining province of Eastern Tyrol.

Since both provinces have a long border with Italy, the Italian influence is obvious. The noodles in the Italian variation are called *ravioli*.

A spot where these and other typically Carinthian specialities are served, is the village of St. Urban, situated on a small but very warm lake called the Urbansee. In the main family hotel the landlady once showed me her cookery book, which is more than 100 years old, and contains many delicious dishes, of which even I, as an Austrian, had never previously heard.

Kärntner Kasnudeln
(Carinthian cheese noodles)

INGREDIENTS for the dough:
500g flour
5g salt
1 egg
1 tablespoon oil
Water as required

INGREDIENTS for the filling:
150g stale diced white bread
1 egg
¼l. (approx. 9 fl. ozs) sour cream
50g butter
½ tablespoon chopped parsley
½ tablespoon mint
½ tablespoon chive
½ tablespoon chervil
500g curds mixed with 50g salt

METHOD:

Mix flour, salt, the beaten egg, oil and water into a medium firm dough and leave to stand for half-an-hour.

Meanwhile moisten the white bread dices with the beaten egg and sour cream. Melt butter, stir in the chopped herbs and pour this over the bread mixture. Finally stir in the salted curd.

Roll out the dough until about an eighth of an inch thick and cut into 3 inch squares. Put a tablespoon of filling in the middle of each and fold to get a triangle. Pinch the edges together and cut out quarter-circles with a pastry cutter (like the sketch shows).

Cook in salted water for about 12 minutes. Drain, arrange on a platter and cover with melted butter.

Serve with *Kärtner Krautsalat* (see side dishes page 144).

Kärntner Fleischnudeln
(Carinthian noodles with meat)

Ingredients, and method of preparing the dough, are the same as for the cheese noodles *(Kärntner Kasnudeln)*. Only the filling is different.

INGREDIENTS for the filling:
200g minced boiled smoked pork or ham
Marjoram
Thyme
Crushed garlic to taste
1 or 2 egg yolks
or
200g minced roasted pork
1 finely chopped onion
Salt and pepper
Chopped parsley
1 beaten egg

METHOD:
Work the ingredients for the chosen filling together, put a tablespoon of the mixture in the middle of each dough square, and prepare like *Kasnudeln* (cheese noodles).

Hühnerbrust ländliche Art
(Chicken breast country style)

INGREDIENTS per person:
1 chicken breast
3 dried plums
1 green and red pepper
3 potatoes
Butter

METHOD:
Bone the chicken breast and make a short level cut into it in order to get a small pouch. Stuff this pouch with dried plums. Rub the breast with salt and pepper or previously purchased chicken-spices, and fry in butter until done.

Cut the peppers into strips, and fry in a separate pan until soft. Meanwhile have the potatoes boiled, peeled and cut into halves, add these to the pan, season with salt and serve together with the chicken breast.

Tiroler Speckknödel

Up the Carinthian Gail Valley (see *Gailtaler Kirchtagsuppe*) the trail leads on into the province of Eastern Tyrol, where right on the mountain ridge it joins the sixty mile stretch of the Karnic Peace Path, now frequented by hikers, but once the scene of border battles during the First World War.

With the rugged summits of the Dolomites in the background, far-stretching green slopes lead up to tiny villages, of which Obertilliach is the most beautiful. Its group of farmhouses, some four to five hundred years old, are built of wood and stone, and each has its balcony decorated with an avalanche of flowers.

It was in just such a spot that I had the best Tyrolean dumplings I have ever eaten. It was a special honour too, because at Mother Landa's place not everyone gets served. The hostess, a courageous woman who brought up 15 children and cared for a sick husband at the same time, only serves drink or food if she likes you. This is a real novelty in such a commercialised era as ours.

The local style of presenting this dish is to serve the dumplings in the soup and provide a plate with lettuce or other green salad as a supplement. The custom is to consume the soup first, then sample the dumplings along with the salad.

Tiroler Speckknödel *(Tyrolean dumplings)*

INGREDIENTS:
100g streaky bacon
100g smoked boiled pork or ham
4 or 5 diced stale rolls
2 eggs
⅛l. (approx. 4 fl. ozs) milk
Salt
Chopped parsley
1 large onion
Flour as required

METHOD:
Fry the finely diced bacon and finely chopped onion in a casserole, add chopped parsley, diced smoked pork or ham and the diced rolls. Fry until all ingredients are crisp. Remove from the cooker and allow to cool.

Meanwhile mix the beaten eggs with milk and a pinch of salt. Pour this over the mixture and add only sufficient flour to get a workable dough. Shape into balls of about the size of a small fist, and boil in beef broth and stock for about 10–15 minutes before serving. (Cut one dumpling in half to check when done.)

Schinkenerdäpfel *(Potatoes with ham)*

INGREDIENTS:
100g butter
250g boiled smoked pork or ham
3 egg yolks
3 egg whites
1kg potatoes, boiled and sliced
⅛l. (approx. 4 fl. ozs) sour cream
Salt
Grated nutmeg

METHOD:
Cream butter and egg yolks until fluffy. Stir in salt, nutmeg and the finely diced smoked pork or ham. Mix carefully with the sliced potatoes and sour cream. Finally fold in the stiffly whisked egg whites.

Grease an ovenware bowl, empty the mixture into it, and bake for about 40 minutes in a medium oven.

Gefüllte Paprika *(Stuffed peppers)*

INGREDIENTS:
8 green peppers
300g minced meat
100g boiled rice
1 chopped onion
Salt
Chopped parsley
Marjoram
1 crushed clove of garlic
40g butter

METHOD:
Cut off the stalk end of the peppers, remove the caps, deseed them and dip each pepper into boiling water before cooling in cold water. Drain off.

Heat the butter, fry the chopped onion without browning, remove from the cooker and mix with the minced meat. Season with salt, chopped parsley, marjoram and garlic. Add the beaten eggs and boiled rice. Stuff the peppers with the mixture, and place them side by side in an ovenware dish. Cover with tomato sauce, (see next recipe) and stew in a medium oven for about 45 minutes.

Tomato Sauce

INGREDIENTS:
1kg tomatoes
⅛l. (approx. 4 fl.ozs) stock
60g butter
100g finely chopped onion
50g flour
Salt
Sugar
1 tablespoon vinegar
1 crushed clove of garlic
1 level teaspoon of paprika

METHOD:
Put the tomatoes into boiling water, leave for 1 to 2 minutes, drain, peel and slice.

Bring ⅛l. (approx. 4 fl.ozs) of water to the boil, add the sliced tomatoes and simmer until soft, then pass through a sieve.

Fry the chopped onion in butter, stir in the flour and gradually add the tomato sauce. Bring to the boil, season with vinegar, salt, sugar, paprika and garlic and remove from heat.

Upper Austria's favourite dish
(Dumplings filled with meat)

Dumplings with a filling of meat or bacon are one of the oldest culinary traditions in Upper Austria. It is a taste which this Austrian province shares with its neighbour, Bavaria.

The story goes that once a Bavarian was offered three wishes by a good fairy; that his first was for a dumpling meal; that his second was always to have enough dumplings; and for his third, he considered the matter seriously before stating that his wish would be "always to have one more dumpling than enough".

In Upper Austria they would understand such sentiments. Soup, followed by dumplings filled with meat, and served with either sauerkraut, warm cabbage or cabbage salad, represents a typical Upper Austrian countryside meal, washed down with beer or cider.

Rahmsuppe *(sour cream soup)*,
foreground centre.
Gebackene Speckknödel *(baked dumplings with bacon)* left.
Mohntorte *(poppy seed gateau)*,
background right.

Gebackene Speckknödel
(Baked dumplings with bacon)

INGREDIENTS for the dough:
500g boiled potatoes
1 egg
1 tablespoon oil
150g flour
Butter as required

INGREDIENTS for the filling:
150g streaky bacon
Salt
Pepper
Paprika

INGREDIENTS for the sauce:
3 or 4 tablespoons milk
¼l. (approx. 9 fl.ozs) sour cream
2 eggs
Salt
Pepper
Grated nutmeg

METHOD:
Boil the potatoes in their jackets and leave to stand overnight. Peel and grate them into a bowl. Add the beaten egg, oil and flour and work into a dough. Dice the bacon very finely, season with salt, pepper and paprika and shape into small balls. Wrap each ball with dumpling dough. Then roll the dumplings in melted butter and fit neatly into a well-greased ovenware dish. Pour over with milk and bake in a medium oven. When the surface gets slightly coloured, mix the beaten eggs with salt, pepper, nutmeg and sour cream and spread this over the top. Bake until golden brown.

G'hackknödel *(filled dumplings)* with Süsses Kraut *("sweet" cabbage),* centre. Steyrer Lebzeltomelette *(ginger omelette Steyr style)* right background.

G'hackknödel *(Filled dumplings)*

INGREDIENTS for the dough:
¼l. (approx. 9fl.ozs) water
Salt
20g butter
250g flour
1 egg

INGREDIENTS for the filling:
1 onion
100g roasted pork
100g boiled smoked pork or ham
100g streaky bacon
Salt
Pepper
Marjoram
1 crushed clove of garlic
Chopped parsley

METHOD:
Bring the water to the boil, add salt and butter. Gradually stir in flour, reduce heat and cook, beating constantly until the dough comes off the bottom and sides of the pot. Remove from the cooker and allow to cool. Then stir in the beaten eggs and mix well. Put aside.

Fry the chopped onion in a little margarine. The meat, ham and bacon then requires to be either coarsely minced or finely chopped before mixing with fried onion and chopped parsley. Season with the spices and shape into small balls. Wrap each ball with dough and boil in salted water for about 15 minutes.

For this type of dumpling the potato-dough, described for the *Gebackene Speckknödel,* can also be used.

Frigga

In the old days the *Frigga* was the classical Carinthian dish for woodcutters. It was prepared in an iron pan on an open fire. However, because the time needed for preparation is minimal in proportion to the tastiness of the result, it soon became a popular snack in Carinthia. But it still tastes best in the open air, — at a picnic for instance.

Facilities for picnicking, especially for the children, are particularly good in the Rossbach Valley close to the Millstättersee. Along the banks of a romantic brook, where one can hike for a whole day, special lay-bys provide the necessary wood to make fires, and indeed everything else needed to prepare *Frigga!* Milk and bread can be obtained at old watermills along the stream which are still used by the farmers.

Frigga *(Carinthian woodcutters' dish)*

INGREDIENTS:
Streaky bacon
Thick slices of cheese
Salt
Pepper

METHOD:
Cut the bacon into strips and cover the bottom of a pan with them. Top with slices of cheese, season with salt and pepper and fry until the cheese melts. Serve with brown or black bread.

Topfenlaibchen

This dish was one of those which the Upper Austrian born Cilli Kittinger prepared for Adolf Hitler. Her cooking expertise earned her a reputation among the nobility whom she served in the early years of this century. She became Hitler's personal cook in 1938.

However, the appointment was not without its frustrations. Her new master turned out to be a vegetarian, and this must have inhibited the culinary skills of one to whom the pleasures of vegetables, flour and potatoes were merely secondary. Nevertheless she managed to do her job efficiently — for as long as it lasted. By 1940 she had voluntarily left Berlin and was back in Austria, because she did not agree with Hitler's ideas. She died in 1982 at the age of 90.

Topfenlaibchen *(Potato croquettes with curds)*

INGREDIENTS:
500g potatoes
300g curds
Pinch of salt
100g flour
1 egg
Cooking fat

METHOD:

Boil the potatoes in their jackets and leave to stand overnight. Then peel and grate into a bowl. Mix with curds passed through a sieve, add flour, salt and the switched egg.

With a tablespoon scoop out portions, shaping each portion into a ball, then press flat and fry in hot cooking fat on both sides until golden brown.

Serve with a green salad. In Upper Austria this dish is also served with apple compote.

Fleischomelette *(Meat omelette)*

INGREDIENTS per person:
100g chopped ham or roast pork
1 onion
Chopped parsley
Chopped chive
30g butter
2 eggs
Pepper
Salt
Grated Parmesan cheese

METHOD:

Fry the chopped onion in butter, add the finely diced ham or roasted pork, parsley and chive, and continue frying for 2 to 3 minutes. Then pour in the switched eggs seasoned with pepper and salt.

Fry the omelette on both sides until cooked. When plated sprinkle with grated Parmesan cheese and serve with lettuce.

Main Dishes

Whilst the Viennese favour boiled beef dishes such as the *Tafelspitz*, in the countryside the *Braten* or *Bratl*, being the roasted version of both beef and pork, is most preferred. However, by *Braten* the Austrian means not only a piece of meat roasted in the oven, but also a fried steak or a joint quickly tossed in butter to give it colour, all this then stewed together with root vegetables or other ingredients.

The popularity of roasted meat in general is illustrated by the old country custom that in wintertime, when almost all the male inhabitants of the smaller towns and villages gather for the *Eisstockschiessen*, or curling parties, on a Saturday or Sunday afternoon, the losing side has to invite the winners to a *Bratl* dinner.

The following recipes exemplify two of the many different ways to prepare roasted meat. The *Mostbraten*, (roasted beef in cider sauce), is a typical regional dish of Upper Austria.

Reindlrostbraten *(Roasted beef country style)*

INGREDIENTS:
2 sirloin steaks about 150g each
50g cooking fat
30g butter
Salt
Pepper
Flour
250g chanterelles
Some chopped onions
Parsley
1 tablespoon sour cream

METHOD:
Salt and pepper the steaks, dip into flour on both sides and fry in hot cooking fat until done. Put into a casserole and keep warm.

Add the butter to the remaining gravy in the pan and stir in the sliced chanterelles together with chopped onion and parsley. Salt and pepper to taste. Fry until tender, add the sour cream and pour over the steaks. Serve with *Kartoffelrohscheiben* (see page 142) and *Specksalat* (see page 145).

Griessnockerlsuppe *(soup with semolina dumplings)* centre.
Reindlrostbraten *(roasted beef country style)* with Kartoffelrohscheiben *(fried potato discs)*, right background.
Gurkensalat *(cucumber salad)*, background left.

Oberösterreichischer Mostbraten
(Beef in cider sauce Upper Austrian style)

INGREDIENTS:
1kg beef (rump or fillet)
50g diced streaky bacon
50g cooking fat
Salt
Pepper
Mustard
⅛l. (approx. 4 fl. ozs) sour cream
1 level tablespoon starch flour
Some dried plums
Some walnuts

INGREDIENTS *for the marinade:*
¼l. (approx 9 fl.ozs) water
½l. (approx. 18fl.ozs) cider

100g finely sliced root vegetables
1 chopped onion
1 bay leaf
Peppercorns
Juniper berries
Savory

METHOD:
Boil root vegetables, onion and spices for about 10 minutes in ½ pint of water. Leave to cool, then add the cider. Pour this marinade over the beef and leave to stand for 2 days in a cool place.

Remove the meat from the marinade, dry with absorbent paper and rub with pepper, salt and mustard.

Heat cooking fat and fry the diced bacon. Add the meat, toss quickly in the fat in order to colour it, then pour over the marinade, cover and stew in a medium oven until tender.

Pass the sauce through a sieve, heat up again and stir in the sour cream mixed with starch flour. Bring to the boil, then remove from heat and add dried plums and walnuts.

Serve with *Kartoffelkrapfen*, (see page 142), brussels sprouts and carrots.

Oberösterreichischer Mostbraten *(beef in cider sauce Upper Austrian style)* Kartoffelkrapferl *(potato nuts)* right background.

Katzeng'schroa

The initiate into Austrian cooking will be relieved to know that this dish has nothing to do with cats. Perhaps the name originated when a kitchen pussy, watching meat being diced neatly, and expecting to be fed, *cried* when the appetising preparation was set down as a meal for human beings.

The first time I tasted *Katzeng'schroa* was at Braunau on the Inn River, birthplace of Adolf Hitler. This old town, with its numerous Gothic buildings, lies about 36 miles north of Salzburg. The Baroque town of Schärding is both its main competitor and its next door neighbour. Both are among the most beautiful townships in Austria.

It was in Schärding that I found a *Gasthaus* with the most extraordinary landlord. Weighing at least 19 stones, he was accustomed to greeting his guests dressed in the national costume, and playing marching music on a huge tuba. For this, and his sense of humour, he was featured in numerous TV shows.

Katzeng'schroa *(Crying cat)*

INGREDIENTS:
500g finely sliced veal
1 onion
30g butter
Salt
Pepper
Thyme
½ bay leaf
Marjoram
Savory
Stock
1 or 2 level tablespoons flour
Vinegar or white wine
⅛l. (approx. 4 fl. ozs) sour cream

METHOD:
Heat butter and fry the chopped onion until golden brown. Add the meat cut into fine slices (not bigger than a coin) and stirring constantly continue frying for some minutes. Moisten with sufficient stock to cover the meat, stir in the spices, cover and stew for about 15 minutes until the meat is tender.

Dust with flour, add some more stock and bring to the boil. Add sour cream and vinegar or white wine to taste. Bring to the boil again and serve.

Serve with *Nockerl* (see side dishes page 53).

Summer-skiing on the glacier of the Dachstein in the Southern Salzkammergut.

134

Gebeizte Kalbsnuss *(Marinated fillet of veal)*

INGREDIENTS:
1 fillet of veal
Savory
5 or 6 juniper berries
¼l. (approx. 9 fl.ozs) wine vinegar
¼l. (approx. 9 fl.ozs) each white wine and water
½ onion
5 or 6 cloves
5 or 6 peppercorns
Fat bacon to lard the meat
1 knob of butter
1 level tablespoon flour
Anchovy paste
Capers
Salt
Pepper
Sour cream to taste
Fat bacon to lard the meat
1 knob of butter
1 level tablespoon flour
Anchovy paste
Capers
Salt
Pepper
Sour cream to taste

METHOD:
Rub the meat with crushed savory and crushed juniper berries. Leave to stand in a cool place for 2 hours.

Meanwhile mix water, wine vinegar and white wine, add the chopped onion, cloves and peppercorns and boil for 15 minutes. Remove from heat and pour this mixture over the meat while still hot. Cover and leave to stand in a cool place for 1 or 2 days.

Remove the meat from the marinade, dry with absorbent paper, and lard. Rub the meat with salt, toss quickly in hot butter in order to colour it, pour over some marinade, cover and stew in a medium oven until done. Baste now and then, adding more marinade if necessary.

Remove the meat from the sauce and keep warm.

Mix sour cream with flour, and stir into the sauce. Add anchovy paste, capers, salt and pepper to taste. Bring to the boil, remove from heat and set down separately from the meat. Serve with boiled rice or mashed potatoes, and own choice of salad.

Legierte Schnitzel *(Veal escalopes with bacon)*

INGREDIENTS per person:
1 veal escalope
2 slices streaky or lean bacon
Rosemary
Marjoram
Basil
Chervil
Thyme
  (all crushed or powdered)
Anchovy paste
Butter
Stock
1 or 2 tablespoons of sour cream

METHOD:
Beat the escalopes until very thin. Nick the edges and salt. Sprinkle with with the herbs on one side. Spread the bacon slices with anchovy paste and put two of them on each escalope. Roll up and tie with a string.

Heat butter in a pan and brown the escalopes quickly on all sides. Moisten with some stock, cover and stew until done, adding more stock if necessary.

Finally stir in sour cream mixed with a level teaspoon of flour. Bring to the boil, then remove from heat.

Serve with boiled rice or *Kümmelkrapferl.* (See side dishes page 142). A green salad or green peas tossed in butter go well with this.

Faschierte Schnitzel *(Minced escalopes)*

INGREDIENTS:
300g minced veal
300g minced pork
1 stale roll moistened in milk and squeezed
2 eggs
3 or 4 anchovies
30g butter
Salt
Pepper
Grated nutmeg
Stock

METHOD:
Mix the minced meat in with the squeezed and moistened roll, the switched eggs and finely chopped or minced anchovies. Season with salt, pepper and nutmeg. Mix well, then shape into 8 small oval fillets about 2 cm. (¾ inch) thick.

Fry the fillets in butter on both sides until done.

Arrange on a platter. Add some tablespoons of stock to the remaining butter in the pan, cook into a thin gravy and pour over the fillets. Serve with *Schlosskartoffeln* and *Grüne Gurken.* (See side dishes pages 143 and 144).

AUSTRIAN SMOKED PORK

A dish known and served throughout Austria is the *Bauernschmaus* or Farmer's Dish. *Garnished Sauerkraut* is one of its many local variations. And of course smoked pork is best if one has the chance to buy it directly from the farmer, instead of at the butcher's.

There is a mountain peasant in Carinthia so famous for his smoked pork that some butchers from the lake region take their pork up to him for smoking. And in the Upper Austrian Innviertel, at the small village of Eggelsberg, it is the local priest who has the reputation for quality.

This man is indeed a cleric extraordinary. Apart from his priestly duties, he runs a farm, and produces not only the best smoked pork, but also the best cider and *Schnaps* (Austrian brandy) in the region. He stores his cider barrels as in a wine-cellar, graded for age and quality, and every barrel containing a special brand.

He is also the conductor of a regional folk-music group, and heavily involved in keeping up the regional traditions and costumes. But as he smilingly admits: "My own food and *Schnaps* give me enough energy and strength".

You can believe him. He weighs about 16 stones.

Bauernschmaus *(farmer's dish)* left.

Bauernschmaus *(Farmer's dish)*

INGREDIENTS:
4 small pork chops
Salt
Pepper
Caraway
2 cloves of garlic
4 slices boiled smoked pork
2 pairs of Vienna sausages *(hot dogs)*

METHOD:
Salt and pepper the pork chops, rub with crushed garlic, sprinkle with caraway and fry in hot butter on both sides until golden brown and crisp.

Remove the chops from the pan, add some stock to the remaining butter and cook into a thin gravy.

Take a platter and put sauerkraut (see page 143) in the middle. Surrounding the sauerkraut put alternately pork chops, slices of boiled smoked pork and sausages. Pour the gravy over the meat and serve with *Semmelknödel* (see side dishes page 52) or *Selchgriessknödel* (see page 143).

Garniertes Sauerkraut *(Garnished sauerkraut)*

INGREDIENTS:
40g lard or butter
80g sliced onion
80g cored and sliced apples
1kg sauerkraut
½l. (approx. 18fl.ozs) stock
1 bay leaf
Some cloves
Juniper berries
1 crushed clove of garlic
¼l. (approx. 9fl.ozs) white wine
4 slices boiled smoked pork each about ¾ inch thick
8 rashers streaky bacon

METHOD:
Fry the sliced onions and apples in butter or lard without browning, add the sauerkraut and the spices, then pour in stock and wine.

Cover and stew in a medium oven for about 1 hour.

In a separate pan fry the rashers of bacon until crisp, and heat up the slices of boiled smoked pork in the same fat.

Invert the sauerkraut onto a platter and garnish with meat and bacon.

Serve with boiled potatoes.

PORK and CARAWAY

Caraway is one of the spices without which, in Austria, roasted or fried pork would be unthinkable. Together with garlic it represents THE spice to go with every pork dish. In the past there was also a certain amount of symbolism associated with the meat and its favoured spices. They were supposed to keep away demons and evil in general.

People afraid of coming under an evil spell put a pot of boiled caraway underneath their bed, and it often found its way into the coffins of dead relatives.

At the same time, there were more mundane and practical uses. Caraway could get rid of fleas, or help to forecast the season's corn crop. A good yield of caraway was reckoned to herald a plentiful crop of corn.

Kümmelfleisch *(Pork ragout with caraway)*

INGREDIENTS:
600g shoulder of pork
100g cooking fat
200g onions
Stock
1 tablespoon tomato purée
Salt
Caraway
Pepper
1 crushed clove of garlic
1 tablespoon vinegar
⅛l. (approx. 4fl.ozs) sour cream
20g flour
1 tablespoon capers
Chopped parsley

METHOD:
Cut the meat into fine slices and quickly fry in hot fat. Add the sliced onion and fry until golden brown. Moisten with some stock and season with salt, pepper, caraway, garlic, vinegar and tomato purée. Stew until the meat is tender.

Mix flour and sour cream, add to the meat and bring to the boil. Remove from the heat and stir in the capers and chopped parsley. Serve with boiled potatoes and a green salad.

Schweinskotelette mit Zwetschkenpfeffer
(Pork chops with pepper plums)

INGREDIENTS:
4 pork chops
Salt
Crushed garlic
Pepper
Caraway
80g butter or lard
Stock
300g. dried plums
50g butter
50g flour
Cinnamon
Sugar to taste
Crushed cloves
Pepper

METHOD:

Rub the chops with salt, crushed garlic and pepper, sprinkle with caraway and nick the edges. Fry the chops in hot butter or lard on both sides until golden brown and tender.

Put on a platter.

Add some stock to the remaining butter in the pan, and pour over the meat. Keep warm.

Boil the plums in a little water for some minutes. Drain, but keep the juice. Remove the stones and coarsely chop.

Heat butter, stir in flour and gradually add the plum juice and the chopped plums. Cook into a very thick sauce. Add the crushed cloves, pepper, cinnamon and sugar to taste, and set down separately from the meat.

Serve with boiled rice or potatoes.

Steirisches Wurzelfleisch
(Pork with root vegetables Styrian style)

INGREDIENTS:
800g coarsely diced pork or beef
Salt
1 bay leaf
2 cloves of garlic
Thyme
400g finely sliced root vegetables
2 finely sliced onions
800g peeled potatoes cut into quarters
1 tablespoon vinegar
2 tablespoons grated horseradish
Chopped parsley

METHOD:

Put the meat in a pot, cover with cold water, add garlic, bay leaf and thyme in a linen bag, then bring to the boil.

Half-an-hour before the meat is tender, add the finely sliced root vegetables, such as celery, parsley root, carrots etc., and including raw potatoes cut into quarters, plus the spoonful of vinegar. Remove the bag with the spices and continue simmering until the meat is tender.

Put the meat, vegetables and potatoes together with the soup in a bowl or soup tureen, sprinkle with chopped parsley and grated horseradish and serve.

Specialities from the Styrian part of the Salzkammergut

Four lakes typify this area of the Salzkammergut, which consists mainly of the region around Altaussee. The most interesting, in terms of contemporary history, is the Toplitzsee, (Lake Toplitz), which can only be reached on foot. Towards the end of the Second World War, when the Nazis, who had preserved the treasures of the Third Reich in the local salt mines, saw that they could not be removed in time to a place of greater safety, many of their most prized possessions were sunk in the Toplitzsee, which is very deep.

This happened mainly with prototypes of weapons, gold and faked British pound notes. Concurrently there was a plan to detonate the salt mines, and blow up all the famous paintings and statues still hidden there. However, some local people from Altaussee, risking their lives, secretly removed the explosives and preserved the art treasures for posterity.

One bright summer morning some twenty years later there was a further episode in this strange story. Thousands of counterfeit British pounds were found floating on the Toplitzsee. The Germans had intended to flood Britain with these false notes, and thereby cripple the British economy. Now the containers in which they had been stored had deteriorated in the waters of the lake, and sent the fake currency floating to the surface.

This incident started a mini gold rush in the Toplitzsee, as hundreds of amateur divers tried to find the sunken bullion, which was also reckoned to be down there in the depths.

But that is where it still remains.

Steirischer Wildschweinbraten
(Roasted wild boar Styrian style)

INGREDIENTS:
1kg wild boar's meat
Salt
Peppercorns
2 cloves
1 bay leaf
Thyme
½ level tablespoon coriander
½ level tablespoon mustard seeds
1 clove of garlic
1 sliced onion
200g coarsely diced root vegetables
2 lumps of sugar
1 tablespoon vinegar

INGREDIENTS for the sauce:
⅛l. (approx. 4 fl.ozs) red wine
⅛l. (approx. 4 fl.ozs) broth
2 egg yolks
1 tablespoon butter
1 level tablespoon flour
1 knob of butter
1 level tablespoon mustard
1 level tablespoon red currant jam

METHOD:

Put the root vegetables, onion, garlic and spices into sufficient cold water to cover, bring to the boil, add vinegar and meat and simmer until the meat is tender.

Remove the meat from the pot, cut into slices, moisten with some broth and keep warm.

Pour the soup through a sieve to get a clear broth.

Mix equal parts broth and red wine, add flour, egg yolks, 1 tablespoon melted butter and red currant jam. Put on the cooker and beat into a thick sauce. Finally add mustard, a knob of butter and spices to taste. Serve with the meat.

Goes well with boiled potatoes.

"Silent night, holy night"

The region halfway between Braunau and Salzburg, *the Oberes Innviertel,* or Upper Quarter of the Inn River, is famous for its rolling hills, deep forests and romantic moorland scattered with warm-water ponds.

Here, at the village of Hochburg, was born in 1787 the composer Franz Xaver Gruber, who would later become famous for *"Silent night, holy night"*, perhaps the world's best-loved Christmas song.

When Sophia Loren stayed there to make a film some years ago, she liked the area and the local hospitality so much that, during a quick trip to Salzburg, she requested to "be taken back to Austria", by which she meant the Innviertel.

Being particularly well known for its hunting traditions, the area would normally have access to the trophies of the chase, and it should come as no surprise that the main speciality is venison, as the following two recipes show.

The village of Hochburg-Ach in Upper Austria. In the foreground the birthplace of Franz Xaver Gruber, composer of "Silent Night, Holy Night".

Rehfilet Innviertel *(Venison Innviertel style)*

INGREDIENTS:
8 small saddle fillets about 80g each
200g chicken liver
100g butter
10g flour
Salt
Pepper
Spices to taste
0·03 l. (approx. 1 fl. oz) Madeira
⅜ l. (approx. 13 fl. ozs) stock
Juice of ½ lemon
Juice of ½ orange
Butter

METHOD:
Rub the fillets with salt, pepper and spices and fry them on both sides in hot butter until tender. Arrange on a platter and keep warm.

Add flour to the remaining butter in the pan and stir in the Madeira. Add stock and simmer for some minutes.

Season with orange and lemon juice. Stir in a knob of butter and remove from heat.

Dip the chicken livers into flour and fry in hot butter until tender. Salt and top each fillet with liver and pour over some sauce.

The remaining sauce should be served separately.

Hirschragout *(Ragout of venison)*

INGREDIENTS:
1kg venison
100g bacon
250g mushrooms
⅛ l. (approx. 4 fl. ozs) sour cream
1 level tablespoon flour
Mustard
1 onion
Cranberries
Lemon juice
Oil

INGREDIENTS *for the marinade:*
Finely sliced root vegetables such as carrots, celery, parsley-root
Peppercorn
Juniper berries
1 bay leaf
1 chopped onion
1 pint red wine

METHOD:

Dice the meat and pour over the red wine, to which the spices and root vegetables for the marinade have been added. Leave to stand in a cool place for 2 to 3 days.

Remove the meat from the marinade, salt and pepper and toss quickly in hot fat in order to colour it.

Add the root vegetables and continue frying for some minutes. Then moisten with the marinade (if necessary add some stock) and stew until the meat is tender.

Put the meat into a casserole, pass the sauce through a sieve and pour over.

Fry the diced bacon, chopped onion and sliced mushrooms in oil until soft, and add to sauce.

Finally season with mustard, cranberries and lemon juice. Serve with *Spätzle* (See side dishes page 53).

Gebratener Hasenrücken
(Roasted saddle of hare)

INGREDIENTS:
1 saddle of hare
Salt
Pepper
100g butter
50g rashers of bacon
Some juniper berries
1-2 tablespoons red wine
1-2 tablespoons sour cream
1 level tablespoon starch flour

METHOD:

Skin the hare-saddle, season with salt and pepper and spread with softened butter on all sides.

Cover the bottom of a roasting pan with rashers of bacon, put the meat on top and roast in a medium oven, basting frequently.

If necessary add some stock.

When crisp and cooked, removed the saddle of hare from the pan and keep warm. Into the gravy stir the red wine and sour cream, the latter mixed with starch flour. Add some juniper berries soaked in red wine before bringing to the boil.

Serve the sauce separately from the meat, with brussels sprouts and *Serviettenknödel* (see side dishes page 52).

Schöpskotelette mit Zwiebelpüree
(Mutton chops with onion purée)

INGREDIENTS:
4 mutton chops
Pepper
Salt
Nutmeg
Ginger
2 onions
Flour
40g butter
⅛l. (approx. 4 fl. ozs) milk
1 egg yolk
Cooking fat
Some breadcrumbs

METHOD:

Stew the sliced onion in butter until soft but not brown, sprinkle with some flour, stir in the milk and cook into a thick sauce. Add the egg yolk, salt, pepper, grated nutmeg and ginger, and put aside.

Beat and salt the chops, seal them in hot cooking fat on one side. Turn over each chop and put a thick layer of onion purée on the sealed side. With the unsealed side in hot cooking fat, bake in a rather hot oven until golden brown.

Serve with French beans, tomato sauce and mashed potatoes.

SIDE DISHES

Kartoffelkrapfen *(Potato nuts)*

INGREDIENTS:
1kg potatoes
2 eggs
Salt
100g flour
30g butter
2 tablespoons chopped onion
Chopped parsley
Cooking fat

METHOD:
Boil the potatoes in their jackets and leave to stand overnight. Fry the chopped onion and chopped parsley in butter and leave to cool. Peel and grate the potatoes into a bowl. Mix with the beaten eggs, salt and flour. Finally add onions and parsley. Work into a dough, shape into small balls, then press flat in order to get discs of the size of your palm and approximately ¾ inch thick.

Fry in hot deep cooking fat until golden brown and crisp.

Kartoffelrohscheiben *(Fried potato discs)*

INGREDIENTS:
Potatoes
Cooking fat
Salt

METHOD:
Peel the raw potatoes, wash them and dry with absorbent paper. Cut into slices about 1 cm. thick, and fry on both sides in hot deep cooking fat until golden brown and crisp.

Krenpüree
(Mashed potatoes with horseradish)

INGREDIENTS:
½kg potatoes
Salted water
Beef broth
Knob of butter
1-2 tablespoons sour cream
Grated horseradish to taste

METHOD:
Peel the potatoes, cut into halves, boil in salted water, drain and mash. Add butter, beef broth and sour cream. Stir in horseradish to taste, and serve.

(Excellent with boiled beef, pork dishes, smoked pork or ox tongue.)

Kümmelkrapferl
(Baked potato nuts with caraway)

INGREDIENTS:
250g potatoes
50g butter
100g flour
Salt
Caraway
1 egg

METHOD:
Peel the potatoes, boil, drain and mash. Mix with butter, flour and salt, and work into a dough.

Roll out the dough until about ¼ inch thick. Cut out discs with a pastry cutter, and put them on a greased baking tin. Brush over with beaten egg, sprinkle with caraway and bake in a rather hot oven.

(Goes well with fried or roasted meat.)

Erdäpfelschmarren
(Potatoes country style)

INGREDIENTS:
½kg potatoes
1 large onion
Lard or butter as required
Salt
Pepper
Caraway
Chopped parsley

METHOD:
Heat lard or butter and fry the chopped onion until golden brown. Add the peeled and boiled potatoes, tear them with a fork into small irregular pieces, add caraway and chopped parsley to taste. Then fry, stirring occasionally until the potatoes form fine golden crusts.
(Excellent with boiled beef, but also any kind of meat dish without a thick sauce.)

Selchgriessknödel
(Semolina dumplings Upper Austrian style)

INGREDIENTS:
2 cups semolina
Half a stale roll finely diced
1 tablespoon butter
2 cups boiling hot broth
(preferably from the pot in which the smoked pork is being cooked)
The dumplings are mainly prepared and served together with boiled smoked pork.

METHOD:
Fry the diced white bread in butter until crisp, and put into a bowl. Mix with semolina and a pinch of salt. Pour in the broth while still boiling hot, then leave to stand for half-an-hour.
Shape into balls and cook for 20 minutes together with the smoked pork.

Schlosskartoffeln
(Castle potatoes)

INGREDIENTS:
500g potatoes
Salt
Margarine or butter

METHOD:
Peel the potatoes, cook in salted water, drain, cut into halves and fry in butter until golden brown.
(Goes with almost every meat dish.)

Erdäpfelnockerl
(Fried mashed potatoes)

INGREDIENTS:
Mashed potatoes
Cooking fat

METHOD:
Prepare mashed potatoes as usual. With a spoon dipped into hot cooking fat, scoop out portions, put into deep hot cooking fat and fry until golden brown.

Sauerkraut

INGREDIENTS:
500g sauerkraut
Stock
120g diced streaky bacon
20g butter or lard
1 large chopped onion
10g flour
Caraway

METHOD:
Stew the sauerkraut with a pinch of salt and some caraway in about 4fl. ozs stock until soft.
Heat butter in a pan and fry the chopped onion and diced bacon until crisp. Add the sauerkraut. Finally stir in flour, bring to boil and serve.
Serve with smoked pork, sausages or roast pork.

Grüne Gurken
(Stewed cucumbers)

INGREDIENTS:
Young small cucumbers
Sugar
Salt
Pepper
Paprika
Butter

METHOD:
Peel the cucumbers and cut length-wise into halves. Cut each part again into halves, then into neat pieces of about two inches long.

Put into a casserole, sprinkle with salt, pepper, paprika and a hint of sugar. Pour in melted butter, cover and stew in a medium oven until soft.

Serve with roasted or fried meat without thick sauce.

Süsses Kraut *(Sweet cabbage)*

INGREDIENTS:
1 head of white cabbage
200g streaky bacon
1 large onion
1 level tablespoon sifted sugar
1 tablespoon vinegar
1 teaspoon caraway
1 tablespoon flour
Salt to taste
Beef broth or stock

METHOD:
Fry the diced bacon in a pan, add the sliced onion and continue frying for 2 to 3 minutes. Stir in sifted sugar, and when slightly brown, add the vinegar, then the shredded white cabbage.

Season with salt and caraway, moisten with stock or beef broth, cover and stew until soft.

Dust with flour and when liquid is all absorbed, add some more stock. Bring to the boil and serve.

(Excellent with boiled or roasted pork or dumplings filled with meat.)

Kärntner Krautsalat
(Cabbage salad Carinthian style)

INGREDIENTS:
500g shredded white cabbage
Salt
Caraway
⅛l. (approx. 4fl. ozs) sour cream

METHOD:
Put the finely shredded cabbage in a pot, pour over with boiling water and leave to stand for 5 to 10 minutes. Drain, season with salt and caraway, cover and allow to stand until cold.

Mix with sour cream and serve.

Excellent with *Kärntner Fleischnudeln*, but also goes with dumplings filled with meat, or roasted pork dishes.

Paradeissauce *(Tomato sauce)*

INGREDIENTS:
500g tomatoes
30g flour
30g butter
Beef broth or stock
Salt
Sugar to taste
1 tablespoon white wine
1 teaspoon vinegar

METHOD:
Slice the tomatoes and stew without water until soft. Pass through a sieve.

Heat butter, stir in flour and gradually add beef broth or stock in order to get a smooth paste. Stir in the tomato pulp. Season with salt, sugar to taste, vinegar and white wine.

Bring to the boil and serve.

Excellent with boiled beef and *Erdäpfelschmarren*. (See page 143.)

Bohnensalat *(Bean salad)*

INGREDIENTS:
1kg tinned beans
1 large onion
Vinegar
Oil
Pepper
Salt

METHOD:
Wash the beans and put into a bowl. Heat up some vinegar mixed with water to taste, and pour over. Add the finely chopped onion and 3 to 4 tablespoons of salad oil. Season with pepper and salt and leave to stand for 1 to 2 hours before serving.

Specksalat *(Lettuce with bacon)*

INGREDIENTS:
2 heads of lettuce
Salt
Sugar
Vinegar
100g finely diced streaky bacon

METHOD:
Wash and drain the lettuce. Pluck into pieces. Fry the diced bacon in a pan until crisp and pour this over, along with its fat.

In the same pan heat up vinegar, stir in salt and sugar to taste, and add to the lettuce. Serve immediately.

(Excellent with all kinds of pork dishes.)

Rotkraut *(Red cabbage)*

INGREDIENTS:
1kg finely shredded red cabbage
1 or 2 grated apples
1 teaspoon caraway
Pepper
Salt
Juice of 1 lemon
80g butter or lard
20g sugar
1 onion
1 tablespoon vinegar
Salt
50g flour
⅛l. (approx. 4fl. ozs) red wine

METHOD:
Mix the finely shredded cabbage with the grated apples, salt, pepper, caraway and lemon juice.

Cover and leave to stand for at least 2 hours.

Heat butter or lard and fry the sugar until slightly brown, add the sliced onion and continue frying until golden brown. Stir in vinegar, then cabbage.

Add some water or stock, cover and stew until the liquid is all absorbed, and the cabbage is cooked.

Stir in flour, add the red wine, bring to the boil and simmer for a few minutes before serving.

(Excellent with duck or goose, minced meat or pork chops.)

CAKES, BISCUITS AND DESSERTS

CAKES

Topfentorte
(Carinthian curd gateau)

INGREDIENTS:
125g butter
375g sugar
4 eggs
1 packet vanilla sugar
Juice of 1 lemon
1 or 2 tablespoons rum
1kg strained curds
6 tablespoons semolina mixed with
    1 packet of baking powder

METHOD:
Cream butter and sugar until fluffy. Gradually add the eggs one at a time, vanilla sugar, lemon juice, curds, rum and semolina mixed with baking powder.

Line a 10 inch round baking tin with foil, pour the mixture onto it and bake in a cool/medium oven for about 1 hour until golden brown.

Leave to cool.

Mohntorte
(Poppy-seed gateau)

INGREDIENTS:
150g butter
70g sifted sugar
Vanilla sugar
2 tablespoons rum
Pinch of salt
4 egg yolks
4 egg whites
170g ground poppy-seed
80g sugar
50g flour
50g starch flour
¹⁄₁₆l. (approx. 2½fl.ozs) milk

METHOD:
Cream butter, sifted sugar and vanilla sugar with a pinch of salt until fluffy. Gradually add egg yolks, rum and ground poppy-seed. Whisk the egg whites together with 80g sugar until stiff, then carefully fold into the mixture. Finally stir in the milk mixed with flour and starch flour. Put the mixture into a round, well-greased and floured cake tin about 8 inches diameter, and bake in a medium-cool oven for about 1 hour. Put onto a platter and sprinkle with sifted sugar.

Mürber Apfelkuchen
(Apple cake)

INGREDIENTS:
300g flour
200g butter
1 egg yolk
Pinch of salt
1 or 2 tablespoons cream
100g sugar

INGREDIENTS for the filling:
¾kg apples
50g raisins
Some chopped walnuts to taste
1 egg
Sugar to taste

METHOD:
Mix flour, butter, egg yolk, salt and cream on a board, and knead into a dough. Leave to stand in refrigerator for half-an-hour. Meanwhile core and slice the apples. Stew them in just sufficient water to avoid burning. Cook until the apples are soft and the liquid is absorbed completely. Pass through a sieve, mix with raisins and sugar to taste. Allow to cool.

Divide the dough into two equal parts and roll out symmetrically. Put one half on a baking tin or round cake tin, spread it with the apple-mixture and top with the other half. Brush over with beaten egg white and bake until golden brown. Allow to cool, then serve with whipped cream.

Specialities from Linz, capital of Upper Austria

If it can be said that the *Salzburger Nockerl* (see page 150) is the Queen of Austrian desserts, and the *Apfelstrudel* its best known delicacy, the *Linzer Torte* can claim to have the longest history. More than 4,000 years ago the Egyptians had a very similar cake which was found in the grave of Princess Pepionk Her-ab from the 6th Dynasty. Despite the fact that this particular gateau improves with age, no one was willing to sample its precursor from Ancient Egypt. But it had the typical criss-cross pattern topping a layer of jam, exactly like the Linz speciality.

More recently the *Linzer Torte* is depicted on the painting of a sixteenth century wedding, and by the early eighteenth century the recipe was published for the first time in a cookery book. Since then its popularity has spread to Germany and Switzerland, where it appears under numerous variations. However, as the other two recipes, the *Linzer Weichselkuchen* and the *Linzer Augen* will show, there are more delicious sweets found in Linz than is generally recognised.

Linzer Torte
(Gateau Linz style)

INGREDIENTS:
140g flour
140g butter
140g sugar
140g unblanched grated almonds
3 egg yolks
Cinnamon
Crushed cloves
Red-currant jam
1 egg

METHOD:

Put the flour on a board and mix with butter, sugar, almonds, cinnamon and crushed cloves. Add the egg yolks and knead quickly into a dough. Leave to stand in refrigerator for one hour. Roll out two thirds of the dough and put into a round cake tin of approximately 8 inches diameter. Spread with red-currant jam. Roll out the remaining dough to about half-inch thickness and cut into half-inch strips. Put the strips in a criss-cross or lattice pattern on top of the gateau.

Brush over with switched egg and bake in a medium oven for about three-quarters of an hour until golden brown. Do not cut before the next day. As indicated, the gateau improves with keeping.

Linzer Weichselkuchen
(Cherry cake Linz style)

INGREDIENTS:
140g butter
5 eggs
5 tablespoons breadcrumbs
70g sifted sugar
Pinch of salt
½ tablespoon cinnamon
2 cups cherries
Butter
Some coarsely chopped almonds for the mould
Sifted sugar

METHOD:

Cream butter until fluffy. Add alternately egg yolks and breadcrumbs. Stir in sugar, salt and cinnamon. Finally add the stiffly whisked egg whites and 1 cup of cherries.

Sprinkle a well greased mould with coarsely chopped almonds, put the cake mixture into the mould and bake in a medium oven.

After 15 minutes add the second cup of cherries, which will soon sink into the sponge. When the cake is golden brown, invert onto a platter and sprinkle generously with sifted sugar.

BISCUITS

Linzer Augen (*Linz eyes*)

INGREDIENTS:
300g flour
200g butter
100g sugar
Vanilla sugar
2 egg yolks
Jam (preferably apricot)

METHOD:

Work flour, butter, sugar, vanilla sugar and egg yolks together on a board. Roll out the dough to about one-eighth inch in thickness. With a pastry cutter cut out discs of about 3 inches diameter. Then use a thimble to cut three holes in every second disc. (These are the *eyes*).

Put all discs on an ungreased baking tin and bake for some minutes in a medium oven until slightly coloured. Take the pastry discs without holes, and spread with jam while still warm. Place the holed discs on top.

Allow to cool, then sprinkle with sifted sugar.

The biscuits can be kept in a tin over a long period without deterioration.

Ischlerkrapferl

In the preface to this chapter I have already mentioned Bad Ischl, the summer residence of Emperor Francis Joseph I and his Empress Sissi. The biscuit which derives its name from that imperial resort is very popular throughout Austria, and like the *Linzer Torte* gets better the longer it is kept.

Because of a life-long friendship between Emperor Francis Joseph 1 and King Edward VII, the latter visited Bad Ischl on several occasions. On one such visit he induced the Austrian Emperor to do what Francis Joseph would never have done voluntarily, – ride in a motor car.

The Emperor had visited King Edward in his hotel, and both agreed on a ride through the Spa of Bad Ischl. What Francis Joseph assumed was that they would be travelling in the royal coach, which was waiting outside the hotel. However, Edward had covertly arranged for the coach to leave, and ordered his car instead.

When they left the hotel a curious crowd was already waiting in front of the building. Francis Joseph was compromised – he could not refuse to climb aboard and so made his first journey in a horseless carriage.

Ischlerkrapferl (*Biscuits Ischl style*)

INGREDIENTS:
200g flour
150g grated walnuts or hazelnuts
150g butter
80g sifted sugar and vanilla sugar
2 egg yolks
Pinch of salt
Cinnamon
250g raspberry jam
Chocolate icing
Some blanched almonds

METHOD:

Mix flour with butter on a board. Add walnuts, sugar, vanilla sugar, pinch of salt, hint of cinnamon and the egg yolks, and work into a dough.

Leave to stand in refrigerator for about half-an-hour.

Roll out the dough to about eighth of an inch, cut out discs two inches diameter, put on an ungreased tin and bake in a medium oven until slightly coloured.

Spread every second disc with jam, top with the remaining discs and cover with chocolate icing. Put half an almond in the middle of each biscuit, and allow to cool.

Desserts

Salzburger Nockerl

This Queen of all Austrian desserts was not created in Vienna. The *Salzburger Nockerl*, as famous as its native composer Mozart, was already being made in the Renaissance era for a certain Wolfgang Dietrich von Raitenau, Archbishop of Salzburg.

An archbishopric for centuries, Salzburg had owed most of its beautiful buildings, like the Cathedral, the Castles of Hellbrunn and Mirabelle and the famous *Hohenfeste*, to its archbishops in general and to Wolfgang Dietrich von Raitenau in particular. It was he who had built most of them.

The Salzburg archbishops were strict rulers whose temporal interests often took precedence over the spiritual. For instance, Dietrich von Raitenau had 15 children by his mistress Salome Alt, for whom he built the Castle of Mirabelle, – and for whom also, it is said, he ordered the creation of the *Salzburger Nockerl*.

Salzburger Nockerl *(Soufflé à la Salzburg)*

INGREDIENTS:
7 eggs
140g sugar
70g butter
25g flour
¹⁄₁₆l. (approx. 2½fl. ozs) milk
¹⁄₁₆l. (approx. 2½fl. ozs) cream
Sifted sugar

METHOD:
Cream butter and sugar until fluffy. Gradually add the egg yolks. Whisk the egg whites very stiffly, and with a kitchen spoon carefully fold them into the mixture, interspersing with sprinklings of flour.

Put milk and cream into a casserole, bring to the boil, put the mixture into it and bake in a medium oven for about 5 to 8 minutes until golden yellow.

With a spoon, scoop big "dumplings" out of the soufflé, arrange on a platter, sprinkle with sifted sugar and serve immediately. When the "dumplings" get cold, they collapse.

Germknödel *(Yeast dumplings)*

INGREDIENTS:
250g flour
15g yeast
10g sugar
Pinch of salt
1 egg yolk
25g butter
Lukewarm milk as required
     (approx. ¹⁄₁₆l. or 2½fl. ozs)
Damson for the filling
Butter, sifted sugar and ground poppy-seed
     for sprinkling

METHOD:
Crumble the yeast into a bowl and mix with the sugar. Add 1 or 2 tablespoons of flour and stir in some lukewarm milk. Allow to stand in a warm place until the yeast rises.

Beat butter and egg yolk, add flour and milk and stir in the risen yeast mixture. Beat until the dough comes off the sides of the bowl. Allow to stand in a warm place for at least 1 hour.

Form the dough into a long cylinder, cut off some 12 equal portions, press each portion flat, put a teaspoon of damson in the middle, wrap up and form into a ball. Place the dumplings on a floured board and allow to stand in a warm place for about 20 minutes.

Put the dumplings into salted boiling water, cover and cook for about 6 minutes. Turn each dumpling over and simmer another 6 minutes until a needle comes out clean when stuck in the dough.

Before serving prick each dumpling with a needle 2 or 3 times to prevent collapsing. Pour over some melted butter and sprinkle generously with sifted sugar and ground poppy-seed.

Milchrahmstrudel
(Milk-cream-strudel)

For the ingredients and making of the dough, see *Apfelstrudel*, Chapter I.

INGREDIENTS for the filling:
6 stale rolls
8fl. ozs milk
100g butter
120g sugar
Vanilla sugar
Pinch of salt
100g strained curds
5 eggs
¹⁄₈l. (approx. 4fl. ozs) sour cream
80g raisins
100g butter
½ pint milk for baking

METHOD:
Moisten the rolls in half of the milk and pass through a coarse sieve. Beat butter and sugar until fluffy. Gradually add egg yolks, vanilla sugar, pinch of salt, the curds, the pulped roll and the sour cream.

Then carefully fold in the stiffly whisked egg whites. Spread the dough with the filling and sprinkle with raisins.

Roll up the dough and put the *strudel* on to a well-greased baking tin. Bake for about 20 minutes, then pour in remainder of the milk and bake for another 20 to 25 minutes. Sprinkle with sifted sugar and serve with vanilla sauce. (See *Buchteln mit Vanille-Sauce*, Desserts, Chapter 2).

Milchrahmstrudel *(milk cream strudel with vanilla sauce)*.

Rahmdalken

In Altaussee, in the Styrian part of the Salzkammergut, I found a regional recipe, which, slightly modified, is known as *Liwanzen* in Upper Austria, where it proves to be very popular.

As we have seen in the preface to this chapter, the picturesque village of Altaussee is not without history. Today it is also renowned as the home and birthplace of Klaus Maria Brandauer, whose performance in the film *Mephisto* won him an Oscar in 1982, and made him an international star.

For those with a hankering after the odd and idiosyncratic, the neighbouring village of Bad-Aussee has also a claim to international recognition. It made the Guinness Book of Records when one of its sons, Karl Traunmüller, employed by British Airways in Vienna, flew around the world in scheduled passenger airliners in three days, stopping at each of the five continents in turn.

Rahmdalken *(Doughnuts country style)*

INGREDIENTS:
100g flour
2 eggs
30g butter
⅛l. (approx. 4fl. ozs) sour cream
20g sugar
Pinch of salt
Butter for frying
Jam

METHOD:

Mix egg yolks, softened butter, flour, sugar and sour cream. Next fold in the stiffly whisked egg whites.

Heat butter in a frying pan, scoop out portions of the dough, place in the pan and fry on both sides until golden brown. Spread every second doughnut with jam, top with the remainder, sprinkle with sifted sugar and serve hot.

Äpfel im Schnee
(Baked apples Austrian style)

INGREDIENTS:
500g apples
70g butter
120g sugar
Some blanched and coarsely chopped almonds
Apricot jam
4 egg whites
80g sugar

METHOD:

Heat butter and stir in sugar. Fry until the sugar is melted and slightly brown. Add 2 to 3 tablespoons of jam, then the cored and sliced apples. Continue frying until the apples are almost soft.

Remove from heat and put the apple mixture into a greased ovenproof dish, top with the stiffly whisked egg whites mixed with sugar. Sprinkle with coarsely chopped almonds and bake until the egg whites get firm in a cool to medium oven.

Gebackene Apfelknödel
(Baked apple dumplings)

INGREDIENTS:
500g potatoes
150g flour
70g butter
1 egg
1 tablespoon sifted sugar
20g yeast
Pinch of salt
6 medium sized cooking apples
2 tablespoons butter for the mould
¼l. (approx. 9fl. ozs) sour cream
2 eggs
50g sugar
Pinch of salt
1 or 2 tablespoons rum
Sifted sugar mixed with cinnamon

METHOD:
Boil the potatoes in their jackets, drain and leave to stand overnight. On the following day, peel and mash potatoes on to a board. Mix with flour, butter, beaten egg, sugar, salt and the crumbled yeast, and work into a medium-firm dough.

Peel and core the apples, cut them into halves and roll them in sifted sugar mixed with cinnamon. Wrap each apple-half into a piece of dough.

Melt two tablespoons of butter in a casserole, roll each dumpling in melted butter, then fit them tightly into the casserole. Cover and leave to stand in a warm place for half-an-hour.

Bake in a medium oven until golden brown.

Mix sour cream, 2 eggs, sugar, pinch of salt and rum and pour over the dumplings. Put them back into the oven and bake until the mixture gets firm. Sprinkle with sugar and cinnamon mixture. Serve hot.

Hasenöhrl mit Hollerröster
(Dessert fried in lard and served with elderberry sauce)

INGREDIENTS:
150g flour
2 tablespoons cream
Pinch of salt
3 egg yolks
1 tablespoon rum
Cooking fat
Sifted sugar

METHOD:
Mix flour and egg yolk with a pinch of salt on a board. Add both rum and cream to get a workable dough. Leave to stand for half-an-hour in a cool place.

Roll out the dough to about ¼ inch thick. Cut out triangles about two inches base length. Fry the triangles on both sides in deep hot cooking fat until golden brown. Place on a wire rack and drain. Sprinkle with sifted sugar and serve with elderberry sauce.

INGREDIENTS for the elderberry sauce:
1 litre (35fl. ozs) elderberries
150g sugar mixed with vanilla sugar
½ teaspoon cinnamon
½ teaspoon cloves
¼l. (approx. 9fl. ozs) milk
2 tablespoons starch flour
2 tablespoons rum

METHOD:
Cook the elderberries with the spices and the sugar and vanilla sugar mixture, using just sufficient water to avoid burning. Continue cooking until soft.

Remove from heat and add rum.

Mix starch flour and milk and bring to the boil. Cook into a thick pulp and add the elderberries. Cook for a few minutes stirring constantly.

Serve separately along with the *Hasenöhrl*.

Hollerkrapfen
(Elderberry omelette country style)

INGREDIENTS:
120g flour
⅛l. (approx. 4fl. ozs) white wine or milk
2 eggs
Pinch of salt
60g sugar
Elderberry blossoms (still on the sprig)
Butter for frying

METHOD:
 Mix flour, wine (or milk), pinch of salt, egg yolks and sugar into a smooth batter. Fold in the stiffly whisked egg whites. Heat butter in an omelette pan, dip each elderberry blossom (held at the sprig) into the batter and fry until golden brown. Sprinkle with sifted sugar and serve.

Steyrer Lebzelteromelette

Last but not least of the recipes in this book comes from the thousand-year-old town of Steyr, which is where I am happy to have my abode. The place I love most is its main square, with a central fountain surrounded by Gothic as well as Renaissance buildings, and narrow cobbled streets leading off in all directions.

Situated at the confluence of the rivers Enns and Steyr, the town had been established as a centre for iron and steel manufacturing even in early mediaeval times, and acquired a world wide reputation for craftmanship. Along with this fame and prosperity came the wealth with which to employ the Italian architects who built the downtown area as it still stands today.

Another section of Steyr's industrial and commercial society which earned itself quite a reputation was a branch of the Ginger Bread Bakers, a profession which unfortunately has not endured the march of progress. The last ginger bread shop, located in one of the town's oldest buildings, closed down a decade ago.

This recipe survives, – not for ginger bread, but for a rather unusual ginger-omelette, – to remind us of the ginger bread tradition.

Steyrer Lebzelteromelette
(Ginger omelette Steyr style)

INGREDIENTS per person:
⅛l. (approx. 4fl. ozs) milk
2 eggs
2 tablespoons flour
Pinch of salt
Some raisins
1 teaspoon coarsely chopped hazelnuts
 fried in butter
½ teaspoon ginger (or ¼ teaspoon cinnamon
 and ¼ teaspoon nutmeg)
Cranberry jam

METHOD:
 Mix milk, egg yolks and flour into a smooth batter, then add hazelnuts, raisins and the spices.

 Finally fold in the stiffly whisked egg whites.

 Heat a knob of butter in an omelette pan, pour the batter into it, level the surface and cover.

 When the omelette is golden brown on one side, turn over and fry the other side.

 Spread with cranberry jam over one half, fold the omelette over and turn on to a plate. Sprinkle with sifted sugar.

CHAPTER SIX

THE WINE
TO COMPLIMENT THE FOOD

Vineyards along the Yugoslavian border.

History of Wine

As already mentioned in the chapter on *The Heuriger,* cultivation of the vine is an ancient tradition in Austria. It goes back to the pre-Christian era, when the Celts planted vines along the Danube.

Vine growing first reached a peak at the time of the Roman occupation. The Roman Emperor Probus, who ruled from 276 to 282 A.D., was probably one of the most active patrons of the wine industry along the Danube and around Vienna.

Archeological findings from this era include, not only Roman wine presses, but also the clay beakers which are regarded as the forerunners of Austrian wine-glasses, commonly called *Römer,* the German word for the Romans.

During the Middle Ages it was of course the monks who became custodians of the rich wine tradition, and passed it on to posterity. Yet there is a document still in existence which confirms that as early as 1137 the Viennese wine-growers already had their own representative body, which would indicate even then a considerable level of production.

There are two types of grape still widely cultivated in modern times, the *Blauburgunder* and *Traminer,* which go back to the 14th century. But it was two centuries later before the first trade manual appeared, under the title of *The Planting, Cultivation and Customs of Wine.* Ever since then regulations concerning vine cultivation and wine trade have existed. It was also during the 16th century that the vineyards of Lower Austria achieved their most dramatic expansion.

With the establishment of the Vocational School of Viticulture in Klosterneuburg near Vienna during the last century, wine growing became a science. After World War II the Austrian wine industry had to be rebuilt, and it was then that it adopted mechanisation and the use of modern equipment. All this strengthened the industrial base, so that today Austrian wine is sold in almost every part of the world.

Austrian grapes and wines

In Austria the grape, and the wine produced from it, are given the same name. From approximately 200 different types of grape that are grown, only 28 are chosen for quality wine, from which, again, the best receive the "Austrian quality wine seal" *(Österreichisches Weingütesiegel).*

Bottles bearing this seal have been checked by an official commission. It is therefore a guarantee of pure quality wine officially tested and strictly controlled.

Austria's highest situated wine-producing village: Kitzeck in Southern Styria.

SOME OF THE BEST AUSTRIAN WINES

White wine

type	aroma	taste
Grüner Veltliner	fresh and fruity	sparkling
Müller Thurgau	reminiscent of Muscat	smooth
Rheinriesling	fragrant and fruity	elegant
Welschriesling	fine bouquet	strong and delicate spicy
Weisser Burgunder	pleasantly scented	full, robust, fragrant
Neuburger	bouquet with soft fragrance	smooth with the smell of nuts
Muskat Ottonel	fine hint of muscat	mild and musky
Traminer	distinctly spicy	full, smooth, round
Gewürztraminer	distinctly spicy	full, smooth, round
Zierfandler	aristocratic and mature	noble, fragrant and robust
Rotgipfler	aristocratic and mature	noble, fragrant and robust

Red wine

type	taste	colour
Blaufränkisch	fruity, medium dry	ruby red
Blauer Portugieser	smooth, but robust	dark red
St. Laurent	fruity, dry, velvety	dark red with a violet gleam

The vineyards

Almost two-thirds of Austrian wine comes from the province of *Lower Austria*. The important viticultural areas and major grape varieties there are:

Krems:
Grüner Veltliner, Müller Thurgau, Rheinriesling Zweigelt.

Langenlois:
Gruner Veltliner, Müller Thurgau, Rheinriesling.

Klosterneuburg:
Grüner Veltliner, Müller Thurgau, Rheinriesling.

Wachau:
Grüner Veltliner, Müller Thurgau, Rheinriesling, Neuburger.

Falkenstein:
Grüner Veltliner, Müller Thurgau, Welschriesling, Blauer Portugieser, Weissburgunder, Zweigelt, Rheinriesling.

Retz:
Grüner Veltliner, Müller Thurgau, Blauer Portugieser.

Gumpoldskirchen:
Neuburger, Rotgipfler, Zierfandler, Traminer, Weisser Burgunder, Blauer Portugieser.

Völsau:
Blauer Portugieser, Zweigelt, St. Laurent, Neuburger, Müller Thurgau.

The township of Krems in the Wachau, for centuries a centre of wine-production.

158

The vast vineyards of the *Burgenland* contribute to the province's varied landscape. It ranks as the country's second largest wine producer and enjoys an especial reputation for its top quality *Spätlese*, or late harvest wines. The main viticultural areas are:–

Rust-Neusiedlersee:

Grüner Veltliner, Welschriesling, Müller Thurgau, Blaufränkischer, Muskat Ottonel, Zweigelt, Neuburger, Weissburgunder.

Eisenberg:

Blaufränkisch, Welschriesling, Grüner Veltliner, Rheinriesling.

Styria

Styrian wines have their own distinctive characteristics. Here are the three important vine-growing areas:

Südsteiermark:

Welschriesling, Müller Thurgau, Weisser Burgunder, Traminer, Muskateller, Ruländer, Muskat Sylvaner.

Weststeiermark:

Blauer Wildbacher, Müller Thurgau, Welschriesling, Weissburgunder.

Oststeiermark:

Müller Thurgau, Welschriesling, Traminer, Weisser Burgunder.

VIENNA:

The vineyards of Vienna extend even into the city limits. Noble white wines come from vines which are cultivated on the south bank of the Danube.

The major grape varieties are:

Grüner Veltliner, Rheinriesling, Weisser Burgunder, Müller Thurgau.

A Styrian castle — restored and used as a *Buschenschank*.

How to choose the best wine to compliment the food

True connoisseurs have always placed great importance upon serving the correct wine with every course of the meal, and because of the wide range of Austrian wines, this presents no problem. For your *Austrian occasion* I would suggest the following:

Salads, trout, ham:
Grüner Veltliner, Rheinriesling, Welschriesling.

Pies:
Neuburger, Rotgipfler – both preferably *Spätlese* or *Beerenauslese.*

Snails and mushrooms:
Blaufränkischer, St. Laurent.

Seafood:
Weissburgunder, Welschriesling.

Pike, carp, salmon:
Weissburgunder, Neuburger.

Fried and smoked fish:
Traminer, Gewürztraminer, Rotgipfler, Müller Thurgau.

Omelettes, dumplings, noodles and cheese snacks:
Neuburger, Müller Thurgau.

Potato dishes:
Blaufränkisch, St. Laurent.

Fowl – chicken, turkey:
Müller Thurgau, Neuburger, Weissburgunder.

Fowl – duck, goose:
Blauportugieser, Blaufränkischer.

Kidney, liver:
Blaufränkischer, St. Laurent.

Boiled veal:
Grüner Veltliner, Müller Thurgau.

Boiled pork, beef, ox tongue and smoked meat:
Weissburgunder, Neuburger, Blauer Portugieser.

Fried veal:
Weissburgunder, Neuburger.

Fried or grilled pork or beef:
St. Laurent, Weissburgunder, Rotgipfler.

Venison, wild hare, pheasant:
Blaufränkischer *Spätlese* (late harvest).

Fresh cheese:
Grüner Veltliner, Welschriesling, Rheinriesling.

Camembert, Brie etc:
Blaufränkischer.

Sweet desserts:
Gewürztraminer, Muskat Ottonel – both of the quality *Auslese, Beerenauslese* or *Ausbruch.*

The quality degrees of Austrian wines:

Austrian wines may only be sold as quality wine, if

a) the grapes from which the wine is produced are of the following officially recognised varieties:

White grape varieties:

Bouvier, Frühroter, Veltliner (Malvasier) Grüner Veltliner, Müller Thurgau, (Riesling x Sylvaner), Muskat Ottonel, Muskat Sylvaner (Sauvignon), Muskateller, Neuburger, Rheinriesling, Roter Veltliner, Rotgipfler, Ruländer, Sylvaner, Traminer, Gewürztraminer, Roter Traminer, Weisser Burgunder, Welschriesling, Zierfandler.

Red grape varieties:

Blauburgunder, Blauer Portugieser, Blauer Wildbacher, Blaufränkischer, St. Laurent, Blauer Zweigelt.

b) the wine has not been mixed or blended,

c) the grapes used originate from one viticultural area,

d) the wine bottle bears an indication of its geographical origin,

e) the wine is good in appearance, harmonious in smell and taste,

f) the wine is true to its grape variety,

g) the *must* weight of the grape juice was at least 15 degrees KMW (73 degrees Oechsle).

Wine called *Kabinettswein* must have a minimum *must* weight of at least 17 degrees KMW (84 degrees Oechsle).

This notwithstanding, Austrian quality wines are awarded different gradings according to the time when the grapes were harvested. They might then be called: *QUALITY WINE OF PARTICULAR RIPENESS AND MODE OF HARVESTING* or *WINE WITH PEDIGREE.*

(Qualitätswein besonderer Reife und Leseart oder Prädikatswein).

Hence if a vintner intends to produce wines which will fall into the following categories – Spätlese, Auslese, Eiswein, Beerenauslese, Ausbruch and Trockenbeerenauslese – he is legally bound to report his intention to the local government wine-office not later than 9a.m. on the day of the harvest, and to report the gathered quantity within 3 weeks after harvest. A state-authorized inspector has then to indentify weight and sugar content of the uncrushed grapes.

The first test of the new wine.

The different degrees are:

Spätlese:

A "quality wine" which must be made from grapes, picked after the main harvest, and in a completely ripe condition. It must have a minimum must-weight of at least 19 degrees KMW (94 degrees Oechsle).

Auslese:

A *Spätlese* made exclusively from the best of the crop, after unripe, imperfect and unhealthy fruit has been weeded out. Minimum must-weight at least 21 degrees KMW (105 degrees Oechsle).

Beerenauslese:

An *Auslese* made out of overripe grapes, or grapes which have been attacked by Botrytis Cinerea. The grapes must originate from the most favourable parts of the vineyard. Minimum must-weight 25 degrees KMW (127 degrees Oechsle).

Eiswein:

A wine made exclusively from frozen grapes, both during harvesting and pressing. The minimum must-weight must be at least 22 degrees KMW (111 degrees Oechsle). An additional quality mark such as *Spätlese, Auslese, Ausbruch* or *Trockenbeerenauslese* may not be used.

Ausbruch:

A wine made exclusively from overripe or noble fermented grapes (Botrytis Cinerea). Grapes which have dried out naturally on their vines. To bring out its natural sugar content, it can be enriched with freshly pressed grapes or wine of the same variety and from the same location. The minimum must-weight must be at least 27 degrees KMW (138 degrees Oechsle).

Trockenbeerenauslese:

A *Beerenauslese* made from noble fermented grapes which have shrivelled up like raisins. The minimum must-weight must be at least 30 degrees KMW (156 degrees Oechsle).

KMW Measurements:

The KMW or *Klosterneuburger Mostwaage* is an aerometer which measures the specific gravity of the *must* determined by its sugar content. The sugar content is expressed as a percentage weight of the *must-weight*. There is, of course, a relationship between KMW degrees and Oechsle degrees – the latter being the more familiar German scale of measurement. A fairly accurate conversion can be made by multiplying KMW degrees by 5, or conversely dividing the Oechsle degrees by the same number.

Flute-player in his national costume close to the Hungarian border.

162

How to store and serve wine correctly

To let the wine develop its full characteristic aroma, it is not necessary to have a wine cellar. A cool corner will do just as well, though the area should be well ventilated so that the wine can "breathe". Need one also mention that the bottles have to be stored horizontally rather than in a standing position so that the cork stays moist and fits tightly? This way the freshness and bouquet of the wine is maintained, because no air gets into the bottle.

Another useful hint is to see that there are no strong smells or persistent odours associated with your storage area, as the wine is likely to absorb these.

Temperature is equally important. One should aim at a range between 47° and 54°F., and for preference this range should be constant, as wine is very sensitive to drastic temperature changes. Storing in a cool, dark, quiet and airy place will preserve the full bouquet.

Basic rules on storage life

Normal quality wine is best between the first and fifth year after harvest; *Spätlese* between the third and tenth year; *Auslese, Beerenauslese, Ausbruch* and *Trockenbeerenauslese* can be stored for decades.

The right temperature at which to serve:

White wines in general:	50°F
White wine of the quality Spätlese and Trockenbeerenauslese:	55°F
Light red wine:	60°F
Heavy red wine:	63°F
Rosé wine:	50°F

Repairing the wooden barrels in a wine-cellar in the Wachau.

163

KNOW AUSTRIA BY COOKING

CONVERSION TABLE

Grams ⟷ Ounces

20 g.	¾ oz.
40 g.	1½ oz.
50 g.	1¾ oz.
60 g.	2 oz.
100 g.	3½ oz.
150 g.	5¼ oz.
200 g.	7 oz.
½ Kg.	17½ oz.
1 Kg.	35 oz.

Litres ⟷ Fluid Ounces

1 l.	35·2 Fl. ozs.
¾ l.	26·4 Fl. ozs.
½ l.	17·6 Fl. ozs.
¼ l.	8·8 Fl. ozs.
⅒ l.	3·5 Fl. ozs.

Gas Marks

120°C	¼ to ½
180°C	4
230°C	8

Oven Conventions adopted by the Author

Cool Oven	120° – 180°C	⟷	(250° – 355°F)
Medium Oven	180° – 230°C	⟷	(355° – 445°F)
Hot Oven	230° – 300°C	⟷	(445° – 570°F)

Historical dinner given by His Majesty Emperor Francis Joseph I in the imperial villa at Bad Ischl on 12th August, 1908 to honour His Majesty King Edward VII.

Participants
His Majesty Emperor Francis Joseph I
His Majesty King Edward VII
Archduke Eugen
Archduchess Elisabeth Franziska
Archduchess Marie Valerie
Archduke Joseph
Prince Leopold and Princess Gisela of Bavaria
Prince George and Prince Konrad of Bavaria
Sir Charles Harding
Major General Clark
Lieutenant Colonel Ponsonby
Major General Duke Dietrichstein
Baron Bronn
Baroness Rodich
Baron Nagel
Baron Lederer
Baroness Bombelles
The Ambassador of Great Britain
Sir M. E. Goschen
The Military Attaché of Great Britain
Duke of Teck
Foreign Minister Baron Ahrenthal
Ambassador Earl Mensdorff
Duke Montenuovo
Adjutant General Earl Parr
Baron Schiessl
Bishop Dr. Mayer
Earl Hoyos

Menu

Rindsuppe
(Clear beef broth)

Krebse à la Bordeaux
(Crayfish à la Bordeaux)

Filets Mignon nach Art des Goldenen Hauses
(Fillet of beef)

Rebhuhn nach alter Art
(Partridge old style)

Pfirsiche à la cardinal
(Peach cardinal)

Käsekrapfen
(Doughnuts with cheese)

Krebse à la Bordeaux
(Crayfish à la Bordeaux)

INGREDIENTS: (serves 4)
24 crayfish
1 medium sized carrot
2 onions
180g butter
Salt
1 sprig of thyme
1 bay leaf
¹⁄₁₀l. (approx. 3½fl.ozs) Cognac
³⁄₁₀l. (approx. 10½fl.ozs) dry white wine
Chopped chervil and tarragon to taste
3 tablespoons tomato purée

METHOD:
Wash the crayfish. Dice carrot and onions very finely and cook slowly in 30g butter until soft, taking care not to brown the onion. Add 50g butter and allow to melt. Add the crayfish, salt, thyme and bay leaf. Fry until the crayfish turn red.

Stir in the brandy, white wine and tomato purée. Cover and simmer for about 10 minutes.

Remove the crayfish, place them in a bowl and keep warm. Cook the sauce until half reduced, add 100g butter, chervil and tarragon to taste and pour over the crayfish.

Filets Mignon nach Art des Goldenen Hauses
(Beef fillets "Golden House" style)

INGREDIENTS: *(serves 4)*
600g fillet of beef
Cooking oil
Salt
Pepper
Fine white breadcrumbs
Cooking fat
Butter mixed with herbs and mustard

METHOD:
Cut the meat into slices about 1½ inches thick. Salt and pepper each slice. Spread with oil and dip both sides lightly in breadcrumbs.

Fry both sides in hot cooking fat until tender. Serve each slice with vegetables and a knob of the butter, herb and mustard mixture.

Rebhuhn nach alter Art
(Partridge old style)

INGREDIENTS: *(serves 4)*
4 partridges
Salt
Pepper
30g bacon
50g root vegetables
½ onion
Some peppercorns
2 juniper berries
¹⁄₁₆l. (approx. 2fl.ozs) red wine
20g flour
⅛l. (approx. 4fl.ozs) sour cream
Mustard and bilberry compote to taste
30g butter

METHOD:
Prepare the partridges and rub with pepper and salt.

Fry the diced bacon, chopped root vegetables and the partridges briefly. Add peppercorns, juniper berries and half of the red wine mixed with water.

Place the partridges in a roasting pan and pour over the sauce. Roast without covering for about 20 minutes in a medium oven, basting frequently.

Put the partridges on a trencher and cut up. Sprinkle the gravy with flour, add the rest of the red wine and sour cream, cook to a thickish sauce.

Add some mustard and bilberry compote to taste and pass through a sieve. Put the partridges back into the sauce, bring to the boil again and serve.

Pfirsiche à la cardinal
(Peach cardinal)

INGREDIENTS: *(serves 4)*
8 tinned peach halves
Vanilla ice-cream
Orange liqueur
140g flour
⅛l. (approx. 4fl.ozs) white wine
2 tablespoons oil
Pinch of salt
2 eggs
10g sugar
1 teaspoon rum
Cooking fat
Sifted sugar

METHOD:
Remove the peaches from the juice, and put into refrigerator for half-an-hour.

Mix flour, wine, oil, egg yolks and a pinch of salt into a smooth batter, add a teaspoon of rum.

Whisk the egg whites with sugar until stiff, and add to the mixture. Spoon some orange liqueur into each of the peach halves. Combine two halves by covering with some vanilla ice-cream. Cover each ball in the batter and fry in deep hot cooking fat.

Put the peaches on a rack to drain, sprinkle with sifted sugar and serve immediately.

Käsekrapfen
(Doughnuts with cheese)

INGREDIENTS: (serves 4)
100g flour
⅛l. (approx. 4fl.ozs) water
50g butter
Pinch of salt
50g grated Parmesan cheese
Salt and paprika to taste

METHOD:
　　Heat water, add butter and salt and bring to the boil. Slowly stir in flour and beat constantly until the dough comes off the bottom and sides of the pot.
　　Allow to cool, stirring occasionally. Stir in the egg yolks and mix well.
　　Place small heaps of the dough on a greased baking tray. Brush with egg yolks and allow to stand for 15 minutes.
　　Put the doughnuts into a hot oven (approx. 220○C) and bake for about 10-15 minutes. Do not open the oven during this time.
　　Reduce the heat to medium and bake for a further 5 minutes.
　　Reduce heat again to cool and bake for another 5 minutes.
　　Remove the doughnuts and cut off the tops. The doughnuts must be hollow inside. Allow to cool, then fill each doughnut with whipped cream mixed with Parmesan cheese, salt and paprika to taste. Replace the top.
　　Serve cold.

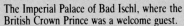

The Imperial Palace of Bad Ischl, where the British Crown Prince was a welcome guest.

INDEX OF RECIPES